The Siege of Colchester 1648

THE SIEGE OF COLCHESTER 1648

PHIL JONES

First published 2003

PUBLISHED IN THE UNITED KINGDOM BY:
Tempus Publishing Ltd
The Mill, Brimscombe Port
Stroud, Gloucestershire GL5 2QG

PUBLISHED IN THE UNITED STATES OF AMERICA BY:
Tempus Publishing Inc.
2 Cumberland Street
Charleston, SC 29401

British Library Cataloguing in Publication Data.
A catalogue record for this book is available from the British Library.

ISBN 0 7524 2552 8

Typesetting and origination by Tempus Publishing.
Printed in Great Britain by Midway Colour Print, Wiltshire

CONTENTS

ACKNOWLEDGEMENTS		7
FOREWORD: A HUNT FOR THE BLOOD OF ALL THE NOBILITY		9
1.	I WONDER WE WERE SO MUCH DECEIVED	13
2.	LIKE A SNOWBALL INCREASING	31
3.	SINNING AGAINST SO MUCH LIGHT	55
4.	THOSE MERCILESSE MECHANICKS	81
5.	THEY WILL NEVER FORGIVE YE	111
6.	CONTRARY TO THE RULES OF HONOUR	131
7.	THAT WHICH HE COULD NOT REPENT OF	153
References		171
Chronology of National Events, 1646–1649		175
Chronology of the Second Civil War, 1648		177
Chronology of the Siege		179
Bibliography		181
List of Illustrations		186
Index		187

COLONEL IRETON: *You being a traitor...*

SIR CHARLES LUCAS: *I am no traitor, but a true subject of my King, and the laws of the kingdom. Sir you ought to prove me one before you condemn me to be a traitor.*

COLONEL IRETON: *We tell you what judgement you are concluded by and that is the judgement of parliament.*

An exchange after the surrender of Colchester (1648)

Warre is a kind of execution of publique justice and a means of maintaining right

William Gouge, Presbyterian divine (1578–1653)

ACKNOWLEDGEMENTS

This book is for the general reader with a special, though not a specialist, interest in history, particularly that of the Civil War. It aims to provide more detail for those curious about the uniquely important, but often neglected, siege of Colchester in 1648 and its role in the wider events of that year which pushed England, with increasing momentum, down the road to revolution.

Much of the detail of the siege itself comes from Matthew Carter, a Kentish gentleman and the Quartermaster General of the besieged Royalists forces. He published his own account two years later. I also rely heavily on the media coverage of the time as it appeared in pamphlets and in news books as they were called – newspapers to us. They tell not only stories from the front line in Essex, but also carry reports from elsewhere in the country: the fate of Colchester – whether or not relief would arrive in time – depended on the result of many actions elsewhere, not least the dramatic shifts taking place in national politics. The newspapers, newly liberated by war from the restraints of government censorship, were fiercely partisan and careful account has to be taken of this when reading such propaganda. But whatever the slant adopted, these tracts tell us a great deal about the priorities, the hopes and, above all, the fears – however fanciful – which drove the decisions of that fateful year. They were collected at the time by the printer George Thomason, who was far-sighted enough see the unique historical importance of the newspaper boom and filed every issue that he could lay his hands on. My thanks to Cambridge University Library for allowing me to peruse their copy of his collection. Reading them may help free us from the curse of anachronistic hindsight and the trap of judgmental assumption.

I would like to thank the Essex County Council's Local Studies Library at Colchester for allowing me to reproduce a sample of the newsbooks and pamphlets in its possession, as well as the marvellously detailed Keymer Map of the siege works, and to let me use their copy of Carter's account of the siege. I am very grateful to librarian Jane Stanway for her help and co-operation and for the advice and local guidance given to me by her colleague, Richard Shackle. My thanks also go to Tom Hodgson of the Colchester Borough Museum for helping to furnish pictures of the principal players in the siege. You can see a detailed list of who provided what in the way of illustrations on pages 184–185. Thank you to Samantha Ponte for donating her artistic talent for map-making and to a trio of erudite friends – Carole Bentley, Rochelle Wilson and Bernard Farrant – who read the script, ensuring its literacy and general sense of direction.

The book started life as an MA dissertation at the University of East Anglia and I remain indebted to Dr Andy Wood for the patient help and understanding he gave me with that project and for the infectious enthusiasm which he communicates to everyone. I hasten to stress that any mistakes in this book are all mine. I have updated the spelling and punctuation when quoting from original material to make it more readily digestible to modern readers. Dates are in line with the modern calendar.

September 2002, Norwich.

FOREWORD

A HUNT FOR THE BLOOD OF ALL THE NOBILITY

It was geography, not strategy, which, in 1648, turned the peaceful textile town of Colchester into a front-line fortress, a decisive battlefield in the final, desperate year of civil war in England. For seventy-five days in that rain-sodden summer, it was pivotal in the ruthless struggle for the future of Britain's political system. Until then Colchester, and East Anglia generally, had been lucky. They had avoided being sucked into the fighting between Charles I and his Parliament, a war which had spread destruction far and wide across the rest of the nation. The townspeople, reliant on the vagaries of the weaving trade, had been more concerned with tackling the problems of economic slump and chronic unemployment. By 1648 the King had been beaten, but the ceasefire, after four years of conflict, brought with it no peace dividend. In the absence of a common enemy, the Parliamentary coalition, tore itself apart.

Like everyone else, the people of Colchester watched with alarm the increasing political instability of the country, the revival of Royalist militancy and the scattered outbreaks of anti-government insurrection which soon ignited a second and even fiercer round of civil war. But they were totally unprepared for the cruellest of all coincidences which placed them directly in the path of two approaching armies. One was Royalist – in retreat but still a large and viable military menace. The other – in pursuit – was part of Parliament's apparently invincible New Model Army. At Colchester the King's men, fast running out of time and room to manoeuvre, elected to turn and make a stand. Thus was the borough, with its entire civilian population, condemned to endure one of the biggest sieges ever undertaken on English soil. Forcibly locked in with the garrison, behind miles of earthworks and trenches, they were reduced to eating cats, dogs and rats to survive: untold hundreds died from disease and malnutrition: buildings were pulverised by shelling and whole districts gutted by fire. Colchester would never regain its prominence as one of the country's leading commercial and industrial centres.

No professional soldier, given the choice, would ever have picked Colchester as a good position to defend in a fight. That decision was dictated by circumstance. One of its defenders was to recall later that it was 'a place never intended for what it was afterwards ordered to do; for it was our first intentions only to quarter at Colchester for a night or two'. Because of its close proximity to the capital, the MPs at Westminster, and the generals fighting in their cause, considered the Royalist rebels in Essex to be by far the biggest threat to their continued existence. It was greater, they conceived, than all the multiple military crises that paralysed the country that year, including the invasion of an army from Scotland. The result for Colchester and its townspeople was devastation.

When, two and a half months later, the victors rode into the town on the morning of its surrender they were appalled by the conditions they found: 'It is a sad spectacle to see so many houses burned to ashes and so many inhabitants made so sickly and weak with living on horses and dogs'. Another reported: 'The poorer are almost famished: many ... cry a penny for God's sake with tears in their eyes.' But rather than treat these afflicted, unarmed civilians as liberated victims of the conflict, Parliament's commanders fined them huge amounts of money for daring to open their gates in the first place to an army of rebels and traitors. Savage treatment was also meted out to of the rank and file soldiers of the defeated garrison. After being promised parole on surrender, they were instead force-marched, in dreadful conditions, across the country, to ports like Bristol, from where they were deported to work as slave labour in the West Indies.

While the lives of the aristocrats who had organised the defence of the town were spared, at least for the time being, two of their subordinates from the gentry class 'were pitched upon' for rougher, exemplary justice. Sir

Charles Lucas, whose family seat was at Colchester, and Sir George Lisle, both professional soldiers, were immediately tried by summary court martial and shot the same afternoon. Neither was allowed to speak in his own defence. Long-recognised codes of honour and chivalry were ignored. Vengeance and the vagaries of a victor's style of justice had replaced them. This savage conclusion at Colchester was a brutal indication of how deep and bitter were the divisions which had opened up within the nation. The war had polarised the parties almost to the point where a slide into revolution had become irreversible. To most moderates it seemed that the government had fallen into the hands of a barbarous rabble, forced up from the lower reaches of society by the anarchy of Civil War.

Royalist propaganda soon turned Lucas and Lisle into the front-line warriors of a rampant class war. There were dire warnings that under way was 'a hunt for the blood of all the nobility and the gentry of England'. The spectre stalked abroad of 'the poor peoples rising up to cut the throats of the rich men'. Three months later an army, under the direct influence of political radicals, staged a *coup d'état.* They purged the House of Commons of all its moderate members, the men they were convinced were about to sell-out their second victory over royal tyranny. One more month and the King was subjected to the pantomime of a show-trial before dying with dignity and courage on the block. The scaffold at Whitehall was hemmed in with Parliamentary troops: the extreme irony of this revolution was that, at the time of his execution, the ceaselessly embattled Charles I had seldom been more popular.

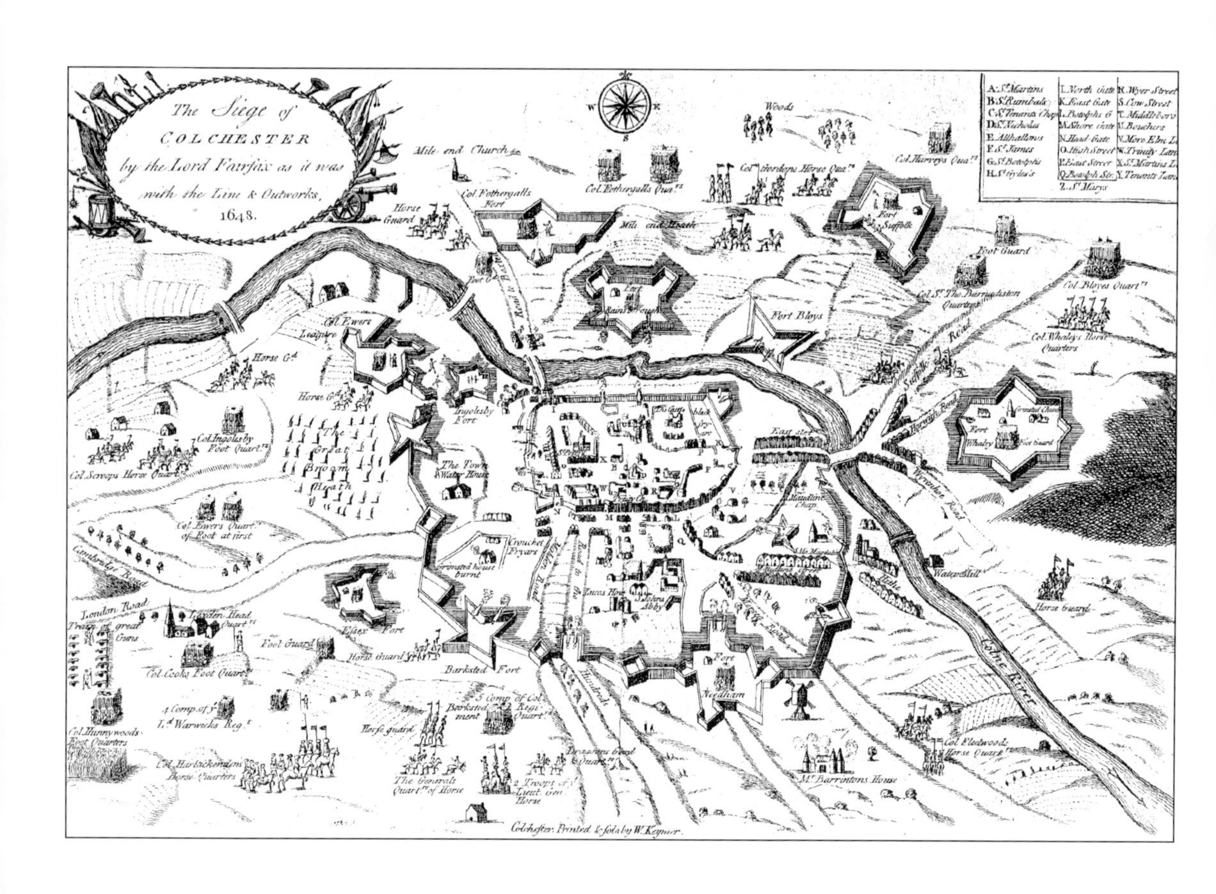

1. The Keymer Map of the siege of Colchester, named after a local printer, shows the huge scale of the earthworks thrown up by Fairfax and the New Model Army to contain the Royalist threat to London. It was one of the biggest siege operations ever undertaken on English soil. (Essex County Council)

I

I WONDER WE WERE SO MUCH DECEIVED

Radicalism and revolution were anathemas to the elite who constituted the political nation when they went to war with their King in 1642. They saw themselves as protecting venerable traditions of government, and their privileged place in its hierarchy, from the inroads of continental-style despotism. In their version the King had to be rescued from a 'Popish Plot', hatched by the 'evil counsellors' who now surrounded him. The aim of these people was to pervert the ancient constitution of the country by turning the monarch, for their own sinister ends, into an absolute tyrant. As far as they were concerned, they were fighting for, not against Charles I – they were no revolutionaries. But wars, once started, tend to take on a momentum of their own and, rather than resolve disputes, have an unpleasant habit of hatching new ones, far darker and more implacable in their implications. After four years of Civil War, the armed forces of Parliament had emerged victorious, but the politicians were inherently incapable of establishing peace and a return to stability. They had, from the start, been a disparate collection of widely varying interest groups; the only thing they had in common was their opposition to the policies of the King, they had no alternative to them. But once the King had surrendered in 1646, the coalition cracked wide open. They could only agree on what they did not want, never on what they did.

The differences which divided them were deep. Now 'peace' had arrived, the money-men in the City of London, who had backed the Parliamentary war effort to the hilt, resented being continually tapped for more cash in order to bail out the bankrupt cause: and threatened a tax strike. The politicians in the House of Commons jockeyed for power in anticipation of how best to benefit from the expected return of the King army veterans, who had not been paid for months, demanded their arrears, while in the rest of the country the general population longed for peace at almost any price and a return to normality. Meanwhile a well-drilled Scots army, which had crossed the border in support of Parliament – and had been a major factor in tipping the battle against the King – was still on English soil and demanding a political settlement favourable to them. They also wanted, as agreed, to be reimbursed for the expense of their timely intervention.

From his captivity the King, convinced that he was still indispensable to the good governance of the country, played a waiting game. He watched the divisions open up between the erstwhile allies, breaches he hoped to further widen by playing off one side against another. He calculated that time, and the still conservative convictions of the majority of people, would help regain his throne. Never did it cross his mind to offer any concessions, particularly when compromise meant dumping the Episcopal Anglican Church for a Presbyterian style of church government. He recalled his father's famous phrase: 'No Bishops, no King'. The clergy would have to stay, mitres and all. In fact religion, all pervasive, all important to seventeenth-century society, was the obstacle against which all attempts at a settlement would founder.

Those seeking the abolition of the episcopacy and its replacement with a Presbyterian State Church – plain, no frills, and ruled by a synod of lay 'elders' elected by the congregations – grappled inconclusively with the Independents, who were committed to a more tolerant approach to worship, one which would even encompass some of the more unorthodox sects that had flourished in the reigning religious confusion. Most Independents asked the question: why should a man not worship as he pleased so long as he was a Protestant? Thus the 'tender consciences that differ not in fundamentals' could be accommodated with room for everyone. They found a staunch supporter in Oliver Cromwell. For many others, though, this permissive talk of toleration was a dangerous invitation to further social division in already disordered times such an open door, according to the Presbyterians would encourage 'all manner of heresies, errors, sects, destructive opinions, libertinism and lawlessness'.

It is difficult for us today, in a Western world where money and material possessions dominate our priorities, to understand the place and power of God in the thinking of seventeenth-century men and women. In a culture where capitalism was newly rooted, the accumulation of large amounts of cash was, for most of the population, a new concept. Consumer goods had not yet replaced spiritual considerations in guiding the lives of the vast majority. From the greatest noble to the lowliest peasant, God was real. Few seriously doubted that the affairs of men were controlled directly by His divine intervention. With such an immediate and inspirational deity, the administration of His kingdom on earth became a vital method of social control for the small elite of powerful men who considered that it was their divinely sanctioned right and duty to rule the rest. In their strictly structured world, custom and tradition were sacred, disrespect for status was considered a potentially lethal threat to the public good; even failure to observe the established etiquette, for example, removing your hat in the presence of your social superiors, was viewed as a significant sign of latent rebellion. Everything and everyone had their allotted place in the hierarchy, and the dangers of deviation were constantly emphasised. As Shakespeare noted a few years earlier: 'Take but degree away, untune that string,/And hark what discord follows'.

In this environment religious conformity was an absolute requirement and evidence of it had to be publicly paraded in a show of good faith, in both the spiritual and the temporal sense. Attendance at the state Church was compulsory. For more than a century that Church had been officially Protestant, or more accurately Anglican, a peculiarly English hybrid, with its bishops, its continued attachment to the ceremonial, its Book of Common Prayer and its virulent anti-Catholic paranoia. Strict laws punished Catholics with exemplary fines and their priests could be executed. Catholic families, some of the grandest in the land, still practised the old religion, but discreetly behind closed doors. They were treated with suspicion, facing repeated and wild allegations of plotting with foreign papist powers. Departure from official state dogma raised the spectre of anarchy, a terrifying word for those who ruled before the days of a police force and without the benefit of a standing army to back them. They lived with the recurring nightmare of insurrection among the great faceless mass of the underclass – that 'many-headed monster'. But there was a worrying challenge from within Protestantism itself to this episcopal stranglehold on the nation's spirituality. It came from the so-called Puritans whose individualistic approach to the word of God, as it appeared in the Bible, was considered dangerously destabilising.

The word Puritan was originally a disparaging term flung at those plainly clad people, all too often ridiculous in their displays of pious simplicity, who campaigned for the constant pursuit of perfection – a kind of rolling Reformation. Puritanism came to apply to a bewildering range of Protestant opinion – conservative in its outlook, as well as radical and sectarian. Many simply tried to apply good Christian principles to their own daily affairs, while the religious fundamentalism of a few sought an official ban on such morally doubtful past times as football, music, the theatre and even the celebration of Christmas. All Puritans sought, in some degree, the promotion of a more godly society, the demystification of Church ceremony and a reduction in the dominant role of the ordained clergy. They urged a more personal relationship with God and a greater individual interpretation of the scriptures, now freely available in English, as well as Latin. Given the sometimes explosive message concerning equality contained in the Bible, the firebrands found themselves straying into taboo territory. By applying scriptural interpretations to everyday politics they were often tempted to criticise the way their political betters were governing them. They began to see themselves as divine messengers, latter-day 'saints', predestined by God – maybe even before they were born – for a place in heaven. This, they felt, gave them a heavenly mandate to direct temporal affairs on earth in the meantime. These modern messiahs were a new and frightening phenomenon for the ruling elite, who depended utterly on the deference of those they were born to govern.

Among all these people, and other less committed Christians, who made up the majority of the country, Protestantism had been embraced wholeheartedly in the years since the mid-sixteenth century. Now many were concerned by the King's recent changes in the forms of Church service: his introduction of greater Catholic-style pomp, his undue emphasis on the role of bishops and clergy and such symbolic alterations as moving the altar table from the middle of the church, where the Reformation had placed it, to the east end and fencing it off to the laity. All these were deeply felt issues which looked like a betrayal of earlier Protestant reforms, a 'Popish plot' to move the Church and the kingdom back into the arms of the great 'anti-Christ' in Rome. And the pope, as every good Protestant knew, was notorious as the natural ally of tyranny and autocratic oppression throughout Europe, a continent now being devastated, for all to see, by the often religiously led ravages of the Thirty Years War. Were all these religious innovations merely part of a plan to turn the King into an absolute monarch? It was a question being asked by increasingly large and powerful sections of his aristocracy and gentry who were afraid of being sidelined by the process.

These shifts in religious thinking were inextricably linked to changing economic, social and political patterns. Encroaching capitalism, the relentless expansion to a money-based economy, helped to create an expanding social strata, known as the 'middling sort' – artisans, wealthy farmers, professionals and a gathering bourgeoisie, urban-orientated and sited somewhere below the ranks of the gentry. Such people began to influence affairs of state and an increasing number of this 'inferior sort' pushed to be included in the once exclusive ranks of the political nation. However, before 1640 few in these bewildering times would have claimed to represent anything but traditional values and both sides of the hardening pre-war divide claimed to be acting in the defence of custom and tradition. It was the King, said his critics, who had broken with tradition for more than a decade by ruling the country without once consulting Parliament; Parliament, according to staunch Royalists, was challenging the King's divine right to exercise his traditional prerogative to rule the realm. When the shooting war started in 1642, Parliament claimed to be fighting not against the King, but against the evil advisers surrounding him: the Royalists said they were defending the monarch against those social and religious radicals bent on robbing him of his role as the head of the nation. Both claimed, with equal conviction, to be on the side of monarchy.

But four years of Civil War had settled nothing, only created a welter of fresh problems and thrown into the equation a powerful and, to most people, a sinister new factor – the New Model Army. Since its inception the army had never lost a battle: it was well-drilled, combat-hardened and morally motivated and it was recruited in the main from the dreaded underclass. It was to prove the only force capable of stemming the nation's growing disorder and before these determined veterans the traditional ruling classes quailed.

THE ARMY

The Great Civil War in England was bitter, sordid and brutal, nothing like the romantic Cavalier-Roundhead duel of sanitised legend. Isolated incidents of old world chivalry did surface among the officer class, many of whom knew each other very well socially. For instance, William Waller sent

2. Prince Rupert of the Rhine, the King's nephew and one of his principal cavalry commanders: he, and professional soldiers like him on both sides, imported all the latest military techniques learned in the European wars. The siege of Colchester was on the scale of a continental campaign rather than an English one.

a note to his 'noble friend Sir Ralph Hopton' before they fought each other in 1643. He assured him that 'My affection to you is unchangeable, ... hostility itself cannot violate my friendship to your person'. But such chivalry was rare in a conflict which pitted brother against brother, father against son, neighbour against friend, tenant against landlord. 'Manifold miseries of civil war and discord' followed, fortunately nothing on the scale of the Thirty Years War on the continent, where large sections of the landscape had been depopulated and laid waste and where in only one atrocity more than 20,000 inhabitants of Magdeburg were killed as the victorious army went on a three-day frenzy of pillage and slaughter. Many of the professional soldiers who fought on both sides in the various theatres of operations in Britain had been trained in one or more of Europe's endless conflicts, including the King's nephew, Prince Rupert and the commander of the New Model Army, Sir Thomas Fairfax.

The war had savage consequences for civilians. Rival garrisons prolifer-ated leading to widespread and destructive skirmishing across the

3. Lieutenant-General Oliver Cromwell, politician and soldier: he was responsible for the formation of the New Model Army, a modernised, professional and dedicated force designed to win total victory over the King. With the defeat of Charles I it was not long before it began to interfere in the political running of the country.

surrounding countryside. The continental practice of fire raids – denying food and resources to the enemy by putting a match to it – became standard practice. As well as grain and livestock, the military commandeered, 'Dutch fashion', horses, carts and even their drivers, bringing rural communities to a standstill. Some local commanders behaved more like local war-lords, pocketing protection money for the safe conduct of goods and people. Troops of all armies were paid only erratically leaving them no money to buy, rather than simply steal food; their officers often had to stand helplessly by, or join in, to ensure orderly pillaging when their starving men began to help themselves.

It has been estimated that 100,000 people died in the fighting, or from related causes, in England, Scotland and – forty per cent of the total – in Ireland. It was the worst loss of life experienced in these islands until the carnage of World War I. More soldiers died of disease than in battle; one contemporary thought that three-quarters of them were lost that way and, of course, they spread epidemics everywhere they went. Overseas and local trade between districts was disrupted, unemployment soared and commercial contacts, which normally cemented society together, crumbled. The weather too added to the agony; a series of wet, cold summers led to repeated harvest failures, with persistent shortages and rocketing prices.

The temporary peace brought little tangible relief. Bands of idle, unpaid troops from both sides roamed about without purpose; looting, rape and extortion were commonplace; ex-Royalist cavalrymen turned to highway robbery; soldiers from several of Parliament's regional armies unsuccessfully demanded their promised pay arrears and began taking what they considered to be their dues at swordpoint from the civilian population. By the summer of 1647 the country was on the verge of anarchy with serious disturbances reported in thirty-six of the country's forty counties, many of them resulting in armed clashes between civilians and the military. On top of all this and despite the ceasefire there had been no reduction in the sky-high war time rates of taxation, ten times their pre-war levels. Parliamentary tax collectors were even more voracious than those of the King.

The one organisation which continued to hang together in this chaos was the New Model Army. It had been founded in 1644, when Cromwell led the political effort to wrestle the conduct of the war from the dead hand of less than aggressive aristocrats like the Earl of Manchester. The earl's innate caution, verging on defeatism, appalled all those committed to an outright military victory over the King. Cromwell had been amazed and furious when he heard Manchester's philosophy: 'If we beat the King ninety and nine times he would be King still,... and we subjects still; but if he beat us but once we should be hanged, and our posterity undone'. Cromwell had never made any bones about which sort of men he preferred to command: 'I had rather had a plain russet-coated captain that knows what he fights for and lives what he knows, than that which you call a gentleman and is nothing else'. Using his influence in the House of Commons, Cromwell helped with the passage of the Self Denying Ordinance which forced the replacement of the likes of Manchester by professional and experienced soldiers made of sterner stuff, by those not afraid to go for a quick, decisive military result. The army was re-organised and a modern New Model Army, incorporating all the latest tactical thinking, was formed with Sir Thomas Fairfax as its commander-in-chief. He was a seasoned soldier of skill and daring, popular with the men and acceptable to a wide range of Parliamentary factions.

The New Model Army quickly proved its worth, particularly at the decisive battle of Naseby in June 1645, which marked the beginning of the

4. Sir Thomas Fairfax, commander-in-chief of the New Model Army: he was a talented, courageous and chivalrous commander, but also had the added attraction of being a political moderate acceptable to a wide cross-section of opinion within the fractious Parliamentary movement.

end for the Royalist cause. It was never defeated for several reasons: as well as being expertly trained, it was equipped with the latest weaponry, was well-clothed and fed and was undoubtedly helped by the continual tactical blunders of the other side. Its leaders were militarily competent, free from political interference and genuinely concerned with the welfare of their men. Thanks too to the superior financial organisation of Parliament, the troops were paid regularly. This worked well in two ways: it boosted morale and made them popular among the civilian population. When they commandeered goods and services they paid for them in full. Strict discipline and an energetic religious motivation put an end to plunder and drunkenness among the rank and file.

That the New Model Army was never beaten in battle was proof enough for its men that their mission enjoyed divine approval – they were an army of self appointed 'Saints'. *Esprit de corps* was high. Hymns and psalms formed part of their armoury and their religious zeal in battle made them savagely single-minded as they went about the merciless work of slaughtering the ungodly opposition. Cromwell, described his almost spiritual ecstasy before combat in these words:

> I could (riding alone about my business) but smile out to God in praises, in assurance of victory, because God would by things that are not, bring to naught things that are. Of which I had great assurance; and God did it.

He praised the new force for its camaraderie, born of religious toleration:

> Presbyterians, Independents, all have here the same spirit of faith and prayer; they all agree here, know no names of difference; pity it is it should be otherwise anywhere.

The New Model Army was unique, and this was to have profound effects on the future government of Britain. In its ranks a soldier's social origins counted for nothing; he was valued for his fighting skills, regardless of class. The conviction of the troops in the righteousness of their cause, coupled with their rigid discipline, developed in them powerful military muscles which would eventually, and almost inevitably, lead them directly into the centre of the political arena.

THE KING DEFEATED

By April 1646, it was clear that the war was effectively over. Parliament had won. Only a few outposts of Royalism fought on with increasing desperation. At three o' clock on the morning of 26 April the King, disguised as a servant, his elegant beard cropped close to his chin and taking with him only two of his most trustworthy courtiers, slipped secretly out of Oxford. The town had been his capital for most of the Civil War, but now the forces of Parliament closed about it for the kill. Charles left behind the bulk of his quarrelsome entourage, still bickering among themselves about which faction should control their doomed cause. The King may have at last been forced to admit the reality of military defeat, but he had not the slightest intention of ever surrendering his monarchical rights and privileges; he had inherited them by divine right and no man could take them away. This principle, to the despair of his more moderate supporters, was still non-negotiable despite four years of fighting which had decimated his armies and wrecked large areas of his realm. As he rode over Magdalen Bridge and the gates of the town swung to behind him, it is probable that the fugitive King was still debating exactly what to do next.

There were three immediate options. He could go underground to continue the fight. He was still able to believe, in the face of all the evidence, that a country sick of slaughter would be only too anxious to put a stop to it and settle on his terms. On the other hand, he could take a boat into exile and enlist foreign aid from Cardinal Mazarin in France – his French wife Henrietta Maria was still tirelessly campaigning on his behalf in Paris. Or he could give himself up to the Scots army, now besieging Newark in Nottinghamshire: they were falling out with their Parliamentary confederates who they had rushed in to support two years before. The covenant made then between the two parties was beginning to wear thin. With victory approaching the Scots were demanding to be paid, as agreed, for services rendered to the Parliamentary cause. The Scots also wanted, as per agreement, a Presbyterian Church structure, modelled on their own, to be adopted as the state religion of England.

But Charles was still their King too and was well aware of his potential value to them, particularly as their government back home was now facing serious domestic rebellion. Confident that his regal charisma still counted for something, he was convinced that the Scots Covenanters could be manipulated to his own advantage. Surely the widening split between them and the English Parliament was ripe for exploitation. Despite his contempt for them – 'abominable relapsed rogues' according to him – he sought refuge there.

Charles had crept out of Oxford accompanied by the staunch soldier-courtier, John Ashburnham, and one of the royal chaplains, Dr Hudson, a cleric with a taste for danger and intrigue. The trio made their way in a long, clandestine loop, through Berkshire, Hertfordshire and East Anglia to Newark, bribing and bluffing their way through road blocks and waving forged travel permits purportedly signed by Sir Thomas Fairfax, commander-in-chief of the New Model Army. They arrived unannounced at Southwell at seven in the morning of 5 May. The King considered himself an honoured guest of the Scots army – they thought him their prisoner. But never once did the King offer any concessions. Quite the reverse: his dogged, often solitary and always devious schemes to reclaim his throne very nearly succeeded, but not before the country was dragged into a second round of bloodletting which was to shake its social foundations to the core.

THE EVENTS OF 1647

By Christmas 1646, it had become clear to the Scots that their royal prisoner had no intention of coming to terms with them. He was playing nothing more than a waiting game, so they decided to cut their losses and sell him to the English Parliament. For £400,000 they also agreed to wipe England's financial slate clean and go home, where they were urgently needed to defend the Covenanter-dominated parliament from rebellion: their own civil war with Royalist-backed factions in the Highlands had taken a turn for the worse. The first instalment was paid by the English at the end of January 1647 when the Scots garrison marched out of Newcastle; the rest was handed over on 3 February, when they finally crossed the border, going north. The King was immediately moved to Holmby House in Lincolnshire, considered to be a more politically dependable county by the Presbyterians who now dominated the House of Commons. Their plan was to settle with him and, after disbanding the New Model Army, use him to consolidate their hold on government. But they had miscalculated on both counts. The King had no more intention of being forced into accepting a Presbyterian Church from them than he had from the Scots. The army was also adamant that it was never going home without its pay. The troops were owed at least three months money and were well aware that if they were demobilised and scattered or, as the Presbyterian Parliament also planned, were sent on active service to Ireland they would never get their cash.

Parliament could have achieved a quick and peaceful solution to the situation by coming up with the cash, but no-one was prepared to put the squeeze, once more, on a country beggared by war. Even the parsimonious financiers and merchants of the still rich City of London, where Presbyterian support was at its strongest, were unwilling to find such a sizeable sum. By March the soldiers, still unpaid, sent petitions of complaint from their regiments to Commander-in-Chief Fairfax. They were discussed by the army's council of war, who passed them directly to Parliament. The MPs refused even to read them. Instead they provocatively branded the signatories 'enemies of the state' and repeated their orders for them to disband There was fury in the ranks and murmurs of mutiny. Each regiment elected its own agents, or 'agitators' as they were known, to air their grievances at the council of war The Presbyterians in the House of Commons, they said, were stabbing them in the back after they had risked their lives in the cause and won the war for them. At a rendezvous of troops on 5 June they swore never to disband until they had received full redress for all their grievances These included a guarantee of indemnity from legal action for everything that had taken place on active duty, while they were fighting for this ungrateful Parliament.

A small core of militant junior officers decided to back their demands with some immediate and extreme action of their own. They hijacked the King from his Parliamentary gaolers at Holmby House. A detachment of heavily armed troopers, led by Colonel George Joyce, took the royal guards by surprise. When Joyce was asked by the King for his warrant, he turned in his saddle and merely waved an arm towards his men. 'It is', said Charles, 'as fair a commission and as well written as any I have seen in a long while'. He then rode off with them to army headquarters at Newmarket. Colonel Joyce had acted without the specific or written permission of his most senior officers, but they knew about it and approved. The generals were beginning to lose their grip on the ever-more turbulent ranks. Ominously, the unity of the New Model Army was beginning to break down, while in the countryside the population was being increasingly terrorised by bands of idle, unpaid soldiers from other units.

Events in London now wound-up the tension even further. On 26 July there was an attempted Presbyterian coup in the city. Mobs of disbanded soldiers, backed by unruly apprentices, invaded Parliament and ordered the members, at swordpoint, to vote for them to be given their pay. One hundred MPs fled in the confusion to the safety of the New Model Army at St Albans, providing Fairfax with the excuse he needed to invade London. By the time he got there opposition had melted away. Army discipline was impeccable throughout. Anxious not to appear an occupation force, it retired five miles out of town, to rural Putney, there to await developments – its brooding presence within easy striking distance.

Since early summer the New Model Army had become increasingly politicised under the influence of radical pressure groups like the Levellers whose influence among the men, and the agitators representing them, was growing daily. They were highly critical of the senior officers, the 'Grandees' as they ironically named them, and successfully promoted their programme of fundamental constitutional reform. This included such dangerous ideas as extending the franchise further down the social scale, abolishing the monarchy and the House of Lords as well as organising frequent parliamentary elections. The details were spelled out in their pamphlet, the *Agreement of the People.* It was this document which formed the basis of the famous Putney debates between the army 'Grandees' and the rank and file. The concepts discussed were truly revolutionary, things like 'the democratical' principal. This alarmed not only the civilian establishment, but the conservatively inclined army high command. Cromwell and his son-in-law Henry Ireton tried desperately to calm things down.

However the debates continued to generate great passion. Colonel Thomas Rainsborough, unusual as an officer committed to the Leveller programme, became famous for his pronouncement that the 'poorest he in England hath a life to live as the greatest he' and no-one was 'at all bound in a strict sense to that government that he hath not had a voice to put himself under'. The other ranks insisted that they had fought the war on matters of principle – they were not a 'mere mercenary army'. The agitator Edward Sexby spelt out their disappointed expectations:

> There are many thousand of us soldiers that have ventured our lives ... we have a birthright. But it seems now except a man hath a fixed estate in this kingdom he hath no right in this kingdom. I wonder we were so much deceived.

Cromwell and the others watched in horror as army discipline crumbled before their eyes. Without it they were powerless to influence the outcome of events. He had already warned his troops: 'If authority

5. Sir Thomas Fairfax presides at a meeting of the army council: it came into being in October 1647 to deal with the increasingly radical demands of the rank and file. It was vital in preventing the New Model Army splitting apart after the first war and continued to shape army policy throughout the deepening crisis of 1648 which finally ended in revolution. (Essex County Council)

falls to nothing, nothing can follow but confusion'. It became very clear that Cromwell, the religious radical, was no social revolutionary. As he was to recall later:

> A nobleman, a gentleman, a yeoman? That is a good interest of the nation and a great one. The magistracy of the nation, was it not almost trampled under foot by men of the levelling principles?

Faced with the Levellers' call to what amounted to revolution, the 'Grandees' decided that the time had come to reassert their authority and close the Putney 'talking shop'. On 8 November Cromwell, relying heavily on his influence and popularity among the lower ranks, moved a motion to end the proceedings and send the agitators back to their regiments. It was passed by an unknown majority, but obviously Cromwell was not the only one worried about the break-up of army unity. Then three days later came startling news which further cemented support for the senior officers – the King had escaped from Hampton Court, where he was being held. Afraid 'of being murdered privately' in his prison – there had been warnings of plots to assassinate him – Charles had made his way down an unguarded back staircase and out into the early evening rain. As it happened, the royal fugitive did not go far, only to the Isle of Wight, where he was again confined, but at least he was out of the clutches of the more extreme agitators who had already labelled him their 'capital enemy'. Cromwell and the 'Grandees' could not have planned it better, and indeed have often been accused of doing so. This latest threat to national security sent the shocked soldiers scurrying back to their units anticipating renewed trouble. Brief Leveller-inspired mutinies at Ware in Hertfordshire were soon put down, mainly by the personal courage of Cromwell himself. He found it necessary to shoot only a handful of ringleaders to reinforce discipline. The 'Grandees' crisis, it seemed, had passed and discipline was restored, at least for the present.

In his new prison at Carisbrooke Castle, Charles played endless games of bowls on the lawn but, behind the relaxed front, he continued his Byzantine and secret negotiations, waiting once more for his opponents to fall out among themselves: through the widening gaps in their ranks he planned to clamber back to his throne. His popularity increased with every passing day of instability. Royal agents reported widespread discontent throughout the country with continued military interference in civilian affairs. The Scots too had re-entered the reckoning to become key players in what was essentially a British game. There had been a Royalist backlash north of the border and the civil war, which had divided that nation just as surely as it had divided the English, had suddenly swung in the monarch's favour.

As early as 1637 a revolution had taken place in Scotland, much earlier than in England, which had curbed royal power. Here religion – a radical brand of Calvinism – and politics had combined to bring to power an oligarchy of nobles, gentry and urban burgesses known as the Covenanters, because of their oath of loyalty to the new Presbyterian-based government. The King had been forced to accept permanent checks on his prerogative powers and this success encouraged similar would-be reformers in England. The trouble in Scotland also stimulated the formation there of a formidable national army which predated the formation of the New Model Army in England by at least four years. And in 1644, when they marched south into England to aid a struggling Parliament, they had 30,000 men under arms – about three percent of the entire population of Scotland. It was not the first time they had intervened during the crisis in the south and it would not be the last.

In January 1647, when it came time for them to leave Newcastle, the Covenanting Scots were again deeply divided, with the more conservative among them gaining the upper hand at home. These included desperate aristocrats, many inclined to the King's cause, who were determined to reassert their dominance in government. Charles, now languishing on the Isle of Wight, could help them do it. They sent out clandestine peace feelers to a desperate King, who now appeared more willing to come to terms with them. The upshot was a secret 'Engagement', signed on 26 December, in which the Scots agreed once again to invade England, but this time on the side of the King. The idea was that once reinstated on his throne and suitably grateful he would commit himself to establishing their Presbyterian Church as the official state religion. If these invaders could link up with the disparate elements in England, who now appeared to be sufficiently discontented to risk open rebellion against Parliament, then the King would have found yet another army to fight his cause. The scene was set for a Second Civil War.

At the beginning of January 1648 it had become obvious that Parliament and the army were getting nowhere in forcing concessions from this duplicitous monarch and, by a narrow majority, the House of Commons voted to break off all negotiations with him. It was known as the 'Vote of No Addresses'. Cromwell, and some of the army Grandees, began exploring schemes to depose Charles and bypass his elder son, the now exiled Prince of Wales, by putting his second and it was hoped more amenable son, James,

Duke of York, on the throne. The scheme was sunk when the teenager managed to escape and join his brother in France.

By now the once-popular New Model Army was being seen as a burden on the English population. People increasingly wanted to know why it was necessary, if the war was over, to face the daily expense of employing all these troops, strutting about, still in uniform and throwing their weight around? In fact, the army high command, well aware of the destabilising effect of so many idle men under arms, had begun to pay off increasing numbers of them, as funds became available. They shed 4,000 men who had volunteered to go, leaving a leaner, more disciplined fighting force. Paradoxically, though, it cost money to be rid of them peaceably, money that could only be raised by more unpopular taxation. The generals were trapped in a no-win spiral: they were losing the race against time. More and more MPs began to make contact with the King on the Isle of Wight, ignoring the 'Vote of No Addresses'. Moves were afoot to bring him back to the safety of his capital to sign a personal treaty, almost on any terms he cared to dictate. For the old soldiers of the New Model Army this was tantamount to the betrayal of everything for which they had fought, but among the vast majority of the country's civilians there was an increasingly militant nostalgia for a return to the half-remembered stability of the good old days: if that meant a triumphant return of the monarch, then so be it. And waiting in the wings to exploit this growing counter-revolution were hard-core Royalists, bitter in defeat and only too anxious for an opportunity to fight their old battles all over again. Even worse for committed Parliamentarians, they watched in horror as some of their most seasoned veterans, whose loyal service in the field had won them the war, went over to the other side.

2

LIKE A SNOWBALL INCREASING

By the mid-seventeenth century Colchester, with its population of more than 10,000 people, was by far the most important commercial centre in Essex, dwarfing the other twenty market towns and 414 villages – 'like a cypress tree among small twigs'. It also rivalled in importance most of provincial England's biggest cities. It had a thriving port which fed the insatiable appetite of nearby London for agricultural produce and fish. On the eve of the siege which was to ruin it, Colchester was described as 'the granary of the county'. It also carried on a brisk trade with the Netherlands and the ports of northern Europe. Its mushrooming size – the population doubled in 100 years – was largely the result of a booming textile industry. In common with the rest of East Anglia, Colchester in 1648, had escaped the full horrors of Civil War. Essex, unlike large areas in the rest of the country, had been comparatively peaceful: it had not had to endure the depredations inflicted elsewhere by the ebb and flow of warring armies. However, its agricultural production had slumped due to of a run of bad summers. The cloth trade, subject in normal times to deep cycles of boom-and-bust, had also suffered with exports badly hit by the continuing war in Europe. High unemployment caused increased social tensions. At the outbreak of the Civil War in 1642 Essex and East Anglia were solidly Parliamentarian. The county became known as the 'first-born of Parliament' for the speed with which it had executed the Militia Ordinance and raised troops for the cause.

Colchester had a reputation for radical Puritanism. Even before the Reformation, in the fifteenth century it had been home to a strong Lollard community, critical of the Church in Rome. In the Catholic repression of 'Bloody' Mary Tudor, in the sixteenth century, twenty-three people were burned there, more than in any other place outside London, which only served to alienate large sections of the population, their law-abiding conformity turning to outright hostility. In the end, the grisly public displays so outraged local opinion that they had to be conducted as quietly as possible with armed protection provided for the inquisitors. By the seventeenth century Colchester had acquired a high Protestant profile: 'This town, for the earnest profession of the gospel, became like a city upon a hill and as a candle on a candlestick'. In 1623 the Bishop of London's emissary was still denouncing Colchester's congregation as a 'factious multitude, who will allow no minister, but of their own calling'. In 1637, the struggle over Archbishop Laud's attempts to put up altar rails was particularly acute in Colchester, the same year that the local polemicist John Bastwick, along with William Prynne and Henry Burton, had his ears cropped and was gaoled for life for his denunciation of episcopacy.

One of Colchester's elected godly MPs to both Short and Long Parliaments in 1640, Harbottle Grimston, became a mouthpiece for the political and religious grievances of the county:

> The church [is] distracted, the gospel and its professors persecuted and the whole kingdom overrun with multitudes and swarms of cater-worms and caterpillars, the worst of all Egyptian plagues.

When the Puritan Sir Thomas Barrington beat the Royalist candidate Lord Maynard in the 1640 elections, his lordship was astounded that 'the rude vulgar people, ... fellows without shirts, challenge as good a voice as myself'. The influence of militant continental Protestantism was also strong due to Colchester's textile trade. The town hosted an exiled 'Dutch' congregation – mostly refugees from the continuous religious strife in the Low Countries – who also brought with them many innovative weaving techniques.

Local opposition to the crown's assertive efforts to rule without Parliament – the Personal Rule of Charles I in the decade before 1640 – often surfaced

6. Sir Harbottle Grimston, the godly MP for Colchester before and throughout the Civil War. He gave voice to many local grievances, both political and religious, before the outbreak of hostilities. (Colchester Museums)

in and around Colchester, but never so stubbornly as over 'Ship Money' – the King's controversial method of raising cash to expand the navy and increase protection for British seaborne commerce. Because it had been levied by royal prerogative, without the consent of Parliament, its legality was challenged in the courts and its collection led to endless arguments with the taxpayers. In Colchester it produced direct confrontation between the Puritan-dominated corporation and Sir John Lucas, head of a prominent Royalist landowning family. The rise of the Lucas family went back to the time of Henry VIII when they acquired, with the dissolution of the monasteries, St John's Abbey, only a stone's throw from the ancient walls of Colchester. Sir John Lucas became extremely unpopular among the oligarchy which ran the corporation, as well as the rest of the population, because of several long-running disputes centred on the town's water supply and public rights to common land. In 1637 he was appointed by the crown as High Sheriff of Essex, a job which entailed collecting the hated 'Ship Money'. Sir John, a staunch and haughty supporter of the monarch, went about the task with characteristic arrogance and zeal. He even, on one occasion, visited the houses of defaulters 'in person and distrains their goods'. He earned a hearty commendation and a knighthood from a grateful King, but a deep, festering resentment from many in Colchester.

That rancour burst into violence in the summer of 1642 when Sir John attempted to send horses and arms to the King, who was by now in the Midlands and at war with his Parliament. A mob of 5,000 besieged his abbey home, looted it and dragged the family and their chaplain into town. When the Mayor offered shelter to Sir John and his aged mother, the rioters threatened to 'down my house upon my head'. Lucas had to be ignominiously locked-up in the town gaol, for his own protection, before being taken to London to be charged with giving aid to the King. He later skipped bail and joined Charles I at Oxford. The trouble he caused quickly spread to the rest of the county and into Suffolk. Large crowds of 'the rude multitude' pillaged the homes of the 'nobility, gentry and others, either known papists or protestants their very houses defaced and made uninhabitable'. Parliament realised that the mobs were a potent check to any further defections to the King's cause, but were caught between having to be seen to disown this appalling break down of law and order whilst taking full advantage of the climate of terror that it generated. Eventually the two Colchester MPs were successfully sent from Westminster to calm the situation. The escalation in the Civil War caused a further government clamp-down, but the violence had by then had a salutary effect on keeping the Home Counties in line. As one contemporary commentator observed: 'This insurrection scareth all the malignant party'.

REBELS AND RENEGADES

In Essex, as elsewhere, the defeat of the Royalist forces in 1646 solved nothing and pleased no-one. There was no peace treaty, the constitutional monarchists could get no concessions from the King, the soldiers of the New Model Army were asking why had they fought at all if nothing was going to change, and the local gentry were still angry at being taxed at premium wartime rates. To add insult to injury, the traditional powerbrokers from the peerage and upper gentry had either been excluded from government, because of their Royalist sympathies, or had withdrawn into resentful isolation, affronted and appalled at being shouldered aside by the upstarts and *parvenus* on Parliament's county committees. These they considered as 'men of sordid condition', who had been appointed during the emergency by Westminster to follow instructions from the centre and run the war effort in the localities. They were thought to be inadequate social climbers,

> a more inferior sort of common people who executed the commands of Parliament in all the counties of the kingdom with such rigour and tyranny as was natural for such persons to use over and towards those upon whom they had formerly looked at such a distance.

They were accused of blatant corruption, dividing up among themselves Church lands and the confiscated estates of Royalists 'while public debts be unsatisfied, the common soldiers unpaid, the maimed unrelieved, the widows and children unprovided for and left burdens on the Commonwealth'.

Parliamentary rule was considered as arbitrary and tyrannical as any practised before the war by the King. Certainly its taxes were higher than his. Royalist news sheets like the *Parliament Kite* or *Telltale Bird* alleged:

> 'Tis money that keeps the Parliament shop open. What honest man hath thrived since this Parliament began? Thousands have been eaten out of their estates by these devouring caterpillars who have purchased large possessions out of the ruins of other men.

Famine and wartime economic depression could be attributed to the punishment of God on sinful people, but there was little doubt that taxation and corruption were man-made disasters. But until 'his majesty would govern by parliament and not absolute sovereignty' it looked as though the victors had won the war only to lose the peace.

Discontent with the regime spread fast, infecting previously solid heartlands of Parliamentary support. Even in Puritan Essex, where they had dug deep into their pockets to support the war effort, disillusion with the lack of a peace dividend cracked the façade of unity. By the spring of 1648 petitions began pouring into Westminster, framed by the gentry of the Home Counties, calling urgently for a personal treaty with the King and an end to military influence in civilian affairs. Significantly the first, containing 20,000 signatures, came from Essex on 22 March. Three months later such petitioning had become so inflammatory that it had been labelled as the next best thing to insurgency. In some places the trained bands, the locally drilled citizen militias, were called out to suppress the activity, only to help organise it instead. Petitioning became a potent weapon of popular protest wielded to great effect by Parliament's alienated supporters among the gentry, who were feeling increasingly threatened by the unwelcome Puritanical dictates of a meddlesome central government. On 16 May angry petitioners from Surrey invaded Westminster Hall and had to be dispersed by troops. About ten were killed and 100 wounded. There had already been outbreaks of violence further north in East Anglia. In April, during the 'Great Blow' at Norwich, the city's arsenal was seized by anti-Parliamentary rioters who then accidentally blew it sky high, killing forty of their own people. The New Model Army was called in to restore order. On 12 May at Bury St Edmunds in Suffolk there was a 'great combustion' of disorder about the simple act of setting up a maypole, a provocative symbol for Puritans of seditious and ill-managed merriment. Things quickly turned political amid shouts of support 'for God and King Charles'. Already, 'in these troublesome and tumultuous times', the trained bands in Colchester had been put on alert as well after alarming reports of trouble from groups of 'malignants'.

Lurking behind this rebellion in the ranks of established Parliament supporters was the far more sinister threat posed by dormant Cavaliers. These old Royalist soldiers were patiently awaiting their opportunity to exploit any flashes of trouble which were spreading, with unnerving speed, from one end of the country to the other. In many places known Royalists were beginning to creep back into responsible positions in government;

they were still being appointed as JPs on the Commissions of the Peace, despite a Parliamentary Ordinance in September 1647 banning them. Behind these civilian supporters of the King, biding their time, were a hard core of military men anxious for a call to all-out armed insurrection. Even more alarming for government was that these hard men were now finding willing recruits among their own ranks, particularly among the officers and men who had fought, often with distinction, for Parliament in the war and were now resentful at facing enforced demobilisation. Some redoubtable old comrades began to defect, their political moderation more in tune with this new, more reasonable Royalism than the hard-line radicalism of the New Model Army and their supporters in Parliament. After all, who was in charge, the generals or the rank and file? For them it was becoming more difficult to tell. All this volatile talk of a universal franchise and a democratically answerable government was a far cry from the modest reforms in monarchy for which they had risked their lives. They agreed with Royalist propaganda which said that: 'The security of the nobility and the gentry depends upon the strength of the crown otherwise popular government would rush in like a torrent upon us'. And they must have nodded their agreement when the following year these fears were spelled out in even more emotive terms: 'As swine are to gardens and orderly plantations, so are tumults to Parliaments and plebeian concourses to public counsels, turning all to disorders and sordid confusions'.

Their worries were summed up by Vice Admiral William Batten. He was relieved of his command after his loyalty to Parliament became understandably suspect during a Royalist mutiny in May among the naval ships moored at the Downs, the important anchorage off the Kent coast. He suffered a very public crisis of conscience when asked to appear before a Parliamentary committee investigating his conduct:

> I remember we fought all this while to fetch the King to his Parliament, yet now `tis made treason to offer to bring him thither; we took oaths to defend the King's person and authority, and now must have a government settled without him and no addresses made to him, but plots and designs to poison and destroy him. These and many other horrible contradictions cause me to abandon these enemies of peace.

It was in South Wales that rebellion within the ranks of Parliament's own military establishment finally took place. There Colonel John Poyer refused to hand over the keys of Pembroke Castle to the New Model Army. Twelve months before he had petitioned Parliament for the repayment of the money that he had borrowed for the wartime repair and maintenance of the fortress while he was the Governor and for additional work on the defences of the town itself. He also wanted the arrears of pay owed to himself and his garrison. Poyer was a volcanic, larger-than-life character. He was described as having 'two dispositions every day' – sober in the morning and drunk in the afternoon. He was soon acting like a local warlord, sending his self-styled 'bullies' out to plunder the surrounding countryside and locking up local dignitaries who offended him. He dressed his motives in more acceptable language when he wrote to the Prince of Wales supporting the King and repudiating the new tyranny of Parliament and its rejection of true religion and the Anglican Prayer Book. The Royalists were well aware of the real nature of their new bedfellow, but bowed reluctantly to the necessity of accepting such men as allies.

Elsewhere in South Wales, in Glamorgan, Major-General Rowland Laugharne, who the previous summer had earned himself the deep gratitude of Parliament for putting down an incipient Royalist rising in Glamorgan, was also complaining about back-pay. His men claimed to be the most heavily in arrears of any of Parliament's armies. There was 'great talk in these parts of the raising of a new army for the King, the Royal Party giving out very high speeches'. Some of Laugharne's men began defecting to Poyer at Pembroke Castle and even helped to drive off one parliamentary attempt to take it back. The Pembroke garrison grew from a mere thirty-six to more than 200, with more joining from all over the region. The county town of Brecon was said to be swarming with 'malignant gentlemen', wearing royal blue ribbons in their hats and shouting 'I long to see his Majesty'. Tenby Castle was taken by the rebels at the beginning of March. What was to become known as England's Second Civil War had started. Only the disciplined professionalism of the New Model Army now seemed capable of maintaining Parliament's precarious grip on power.

THAT MAN OF BLOOD

Much now depended on the nerve and the strategic brilliance of Sir Thomas Fairfax, the commander-in-chief of the New Model Army since its inception. He got the job because his apolitical attitudes and personal integrity made him acceptable to most of Parliament's quarrelling parties.

7. Sir Marmaduke Langdale: he led the Royalist rebellion in the north of England, taking the border fortresses of Carlisle and Berwick. He later linked up with the Scots army of Engagement, which invaded England in support of the King.

He was an instinctive military tactician who began soldiering in 1629 at the age of seventeen in Holland, fighting in a volunteer force for the Prince of Orange. Later he went to France, where he nearly died of smallpox. Known as 'Black Tom' for his swarthy complexion, he was often in ill health with repeated attacks of rheumatism – the Cavalier press christened him 'His Goutship' – but he was saluted by friend and foe alike as a chivalrous man. His deep concern for the welfare of his men made him a hugely popular commander. Fairfax knew better than anyone that he would need all his tactical know-how, a cool head and a strong nerve if he was to stave off what looked like a looming disaster for the Parliamentary cause. One slip now, one tactical mistake, one decisive defeat, or even an indecisive mauling for his army at Royalist hands, could be enough to place the King back on the throne without any meaningful constitutional restraints on his still autocratic ambitions. Wherever it chose to look Parliament was seemingly confronted with insurrection.

By April 1648 the north was at risk as well. Only a few months earlier, committed Cavaliers like Sir Marmaduke Langdale had visited Scotland to lay detailed plans for the invasion of England on behalf of the King by a Scots army of Engagement, as per their agreement on the Isle of Wight in December. Langdale was an incorrigible schemer: in the summer of 1647 he had hatched a daring, but as it turned out impractical, plot to take over the Tower of London for the King and spark counter-revolution in the capital. Now he was to play a leading role in events. In April Royalist rebels took over the border fortresses of Berwick and Carlisle to smooth what they hoped, wrongly as it proved, would be the imminent passage of the invasion army. The problem for Fairfax was how to contain all these flash points at the same time, without spreading his forces too thin and inviting defeat in any one place. It was a logistical, as well as a strategic nightmare. By 1 May he had formed a plan: Cromwell would be sent to South Wales with 'a considerable part of the army', while he, Fairfax, would take a force north to deal with the Royalists on the Scots border. His very presence, it was hoped, would have the salutary effect in deterring the Scots invasion completely. The Engagers in Scotland were already having trouble raising a force substantial enough for the venture because the see-saw of domestic politics there had swung back in favour of the anti-Royalists of the Kirk and the Covenant.

On 7 May Cromwell was ready to go. Time was of the essence, but he paused to attend a prayer meeting of the army council at Windsor. These meetings always found the army at its most revolutionary, but this one lasted for three days and saw both officers and men even more grimly resolute. Before going out once again to do battle, it was agreed:

> That it was the duty of our day, with the forces we had, to go out and fight against these potent enemies and if ever the Lord brought us back in peace, to call Charles Stuart, that man of blood, to account for the blood that he had shed, and mischief he had done to his utmost against the Lord's cause and people in these poor nations.

The implacable mood of the Second Civil War was set; the King was branded a war criminal, the man who bore sole responsibility for what was to follow. He had flown in the face of divine judgement – a very real allegation, not made lightly and profound in its implications. The King, single-handedly, was responsible for leading his country into a second round of bloodletting; he was no longer fit to wear the crown. In this resolution the radicals of the New Model Army shaped the future direction of events: the King was to stand trial for his life. Cromwell set off to besiege first Chepstow, Tenby and then Pembroke in an effort to crush the Welsh rebellion, while the Commons directed 'general [Fairfax]... to advance in person into the north with such forces as he shall think fit, to reduce those places that are possessed of the enemy'. But these instructions were soon overtaken by the accelerating speed of events – an even greater military menace had manifested itself, this time right on Parliament's own doorstep. The formerly loyal county of Kent had also exploded into insurrection. The government had been stabbed in the back.

KENT

The troubles in Kent went back to the previous December when the Puritanical Mayor of Canterbury banned the celebration of Christmas, in line with the increasingly fundamentalist religious policy of the government. 'On the Saturday called Christmas Day', he pronounced, 'there should be no observance of that abolished feast', and ordered the shopkeepers throughout the city to open their premises for business as usual. The offence this caused was almost universal among people who insisted that all they wanted 'was but a sermon'. How could it be that 'that which is good all the year long, yet this day is superstitious?' The shops that opened were soon looted by a riotous crowd. The trouble quickly swelled into a large anti-Puritan, pro-Royalist demonstration when people from the surrounding district rushed into the city. Two days later they took over the county magazine. Things were seriously out of control. The demonstrators, it was reported, were 'in a military and not in a drinking posture'. They remained in command of the city until the beginning of January when, rather surprisingly, they yielded without a fight to the Kentish-trained bands. But the fuse of future rebellion had been lit and smouldered on until 22 May when the whole county finally rose in revolt. Dartford and Deptford fell and the magazine at Rochester, right next door to the Chatham Naval dockyard, was also taken over. The Derby House committee, in charge of the government's military strategy, were told: 'Never was the fair face of such a faithful county turned of a sudden to so much deformity and ugliness'.

Less than a week later the crews of several ships of the fleet anchored at the Downs – at the approaches to the Thames Estuary – mutinied and the castles at Deal and Walmer, whose guns provided protection for the anchorage, also fell to the rebels. The sailors, generally a conservative group of men, objected to the notorious Leveller Colonel Thomas Rainsborough being placed in command. Rainsborough immediately recognised the seriousness of the development: 'the present distemper of the county hath begot

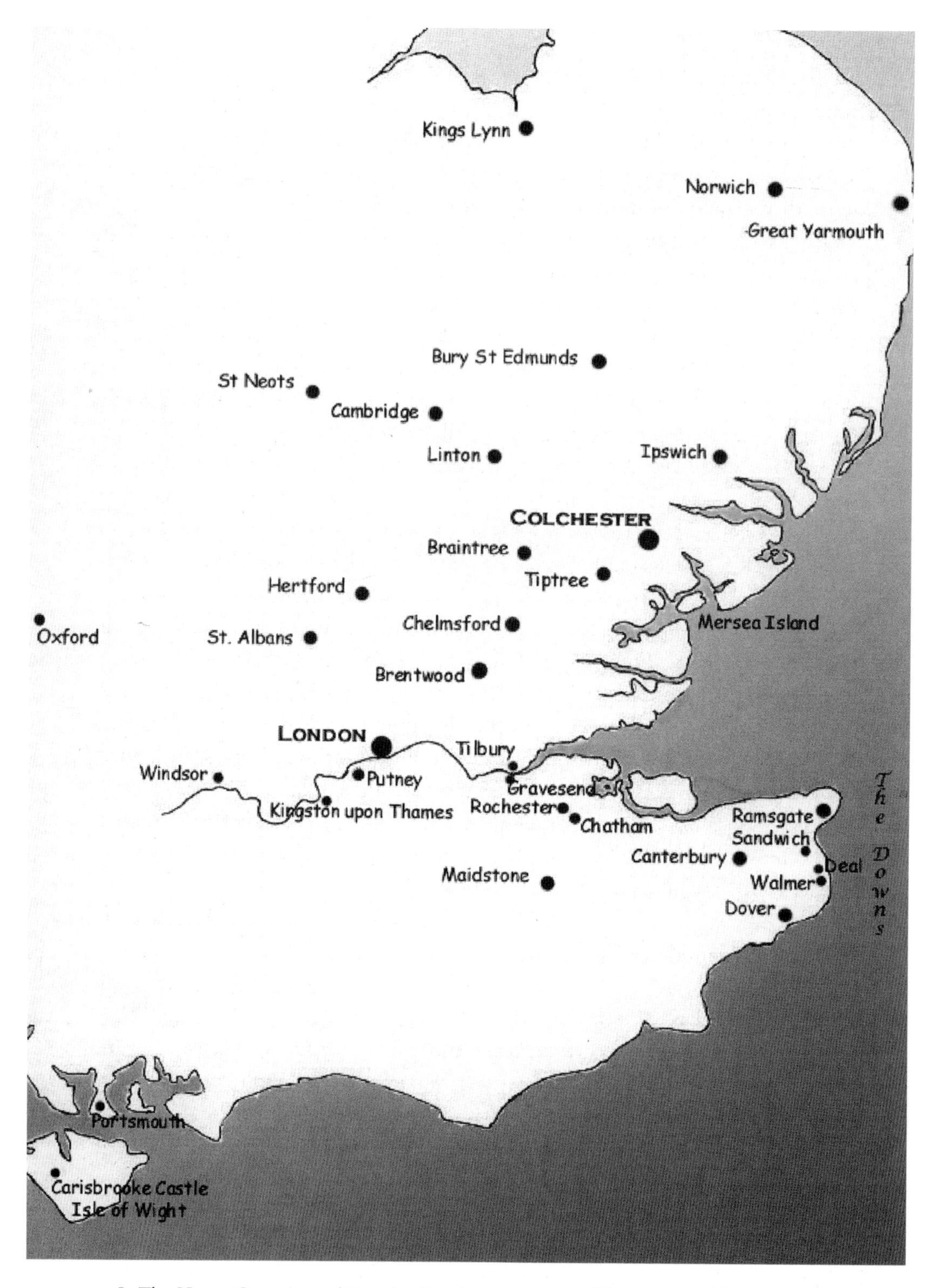

8. The Home Counties and East Anglia, showing some of the main trouble spots in the Second Civil War of 1648.

a distemper in the fleet which will be of dangerous consequences'. The loyalty of the fleet was all that stood between the beleaguered Parliament and a foreign invasion on behalf of the King. Colonel Barkstead told Fairfax on 29 May that the insurgents planned to 'secure a landing for Irish, French or Danes of whose coming they fondly flatter themselves'.

Parliament was dismayed at the speed with which they were losing their grip on events. There were reports that 'very many officers and soldiers that have formerly served the King come in hourly for them'. Royalist militants were hijacking the protest – their aim was to foment all-out war but, as it turned out, the timing of affairs was beyond their management as well. The pivot on which the King's hopes of restoration hinged was an invasion from Scotland. The Kentish insurgency, as all the others, was supposed to be coordinated with that; but the Scots had been delayed and rebellion has an unpredictable habit of creating its own timetable. For the Kentish insurgents there seemed no better time than the present: with the army's attention divided between trouble in Wales, the north and the Home Counties it was generally thought that 'you can never have so appropriate a time to effect your desires'. Even so, many of the great names of the county preferred to stand aloof and see how things fell out. An ageing Royalist leader from another county, the Earl of Norwich – not even an experienced soldier – was prevailed upon to lead the troops. He agreed, with reluctance, to stand in after the Duke of Richmond declined 'the honour'. He hoped, forlornly, that the duke might change his mind at a later date.

Norwich quickly found himself at the head of a formidable army of over 11,000 men and Fairfax was forced to cancel his planned to march north to deal with this far more immediate menace, so near London. Fairfax scraped together all the men he could, despite complaints from MPs that this left Westminster denuded of protection and at the mercy of the London mob. They would have to take their chances with the rest. Even so the Royalists outnumbered Fairfax by half as many men again, but they had divided their forces between Rochester, Maidstone and a siege of Dover Castle. Fairfax avoided Rochester and urgently marched his men by a roundabout route to Maidstone, where the main body of rebels was concentrated. Discipline among his troops was strictly enforced so as not to offend the locals; they were told that they would plunder the population 'at their peril' – they would need all the allies they could get.

The army's advance on Maidstone was so fast, according to Fairfax, that before he had a chance to reconnoitre the town an advance party 'had engaged the enemy and forced them from the ground they kept'. His

A

LETTER

FROM

His Excellency the Lord *Fairfax*
to the Houſe of Peers, upon Munday
being the fifth of *JUNE*, 1648.
concerning all the proceedings in

KENT:

WITH

Severall Papers found in the
pockets of ſome that are now taken
Priſoners, diſcovering the whole

Deſigne,

And the manner how it ſhould have been
put in Execution.

Die Lunæ, 5 Junii, 1648.

ORdered by the Lords in Parliament aſſembled, That the Lord Generalls Letter, with the Papers, be forthwith printed and publiſhed.

Jo. Brown, Cler. Parliamentorum.

Imprinted at *London* for *Iohn Wright*, at the
Kings Head in the Old Bailey. 1648.

---

9. Welcome news for Parliament: Fairfax and the New Model Army had checked the rebellion in Kent. The rising was worrying indeed for the government. The Home Counties had always been considered the heartland of Parliamentary support. A Royalist rising here, right on the doorstep of London, was seen as the most serious threat of all to its future existence. (Essex County Council)

dragoons 'being very forward to engage pursued', but found the streets 'very strongly barricaded'. There followed a deadly round of street fighting, 'through the darkness of the night', from barricade to barricade, but 'after four or five hours hot service' they had secured the place. 'The best of their men were there', Fairfax reported to Parliament, 'whereof many were Cavaliers They looked upon the consequences of that place to be very great and therefore [made] what resistance they could'. Fairfax then turned his attention to the hill at neighbouring Aylesford where 'old Lord Goring [Earl of Norwich], being made general that day, [was] at the head of their army'. His victory there was decisive. 300 Royalists were killed and more than 1,300 made prisoner, 'many of them being taken next morning early, in the woods, hop yards and fields whither they had fled in the time of the fight, amongst them were gentlemen of good quality'. Fairfax reported that 'the greatest part of their army left them and were dispersed', but a hard-core remnant of some 3,000 horse and foot escaped over Rochester Bridge heading for Blackheath. He sent Colonel Whalley after them 'upon whose approach they have left Kent and fled over the water into Essex, by Woolwich and Greenwich'. The chain of events which would engulf Colchester had been set in motion.

THE ROAD TO COLCHESTER

With this defeated, but still intact and highly dangerous force of Royalists heading their way along the south bank of the Thames, the political attitude of London again became crucial. Which way would the city jump? But when it came to the crunch it wavered and once again came down on the side of caution. On their approach the rebels found the gates to the capital barred against them. The philosopher, Thomas Hobbes, was to recall later that at this point,

> Londoners might easily and suddenly have mastered first the Parliament next Fairfax's 8,000, but the city was never good at venturing; nor were they principled to have a king *over* them, but *under* them.

The Republican Edmund Ludlow thought that the city was unwilling 'to espouse the Cavalier party, especially in a flying posture'. The rebels, squeezed between a resistant city and a pursuing New Model Army, were forced, in a state approaching panic, to 'throw ourselves over to the opposite side of the

10. Sir Charles Lucas: the younger son of a prominent local family, he led the rebels to the gates of Colchester. Here they were forced to turn and face the pursuing Parliamentary army. He distinguished himself in the town's defence but, after its surrender, he became a Royalist martyr when Fairfax, uncharacteristically, ordered him to be shot by firing squad as a traitor. (Colchester Museums)

11. Sir George Lisle: comrade in arms of Sir Charles Lucas, he also defended Colchester with great gallantry, only to share the other's execution. Fairfax labelled them both soldiers of fortune who had to be made an example of. (Colchester Museums)

Thames for our further safety' and into Essex, where they were assured they would find 2,000 local men ready to join them. The reality was that the county was in utter confusion. They found their would-be allies unprepared for the speed of developments.

Their approach caused hysteria in the county town of Chelmsford where the members of Parliament's much-despised county committee were meeting to discuss the crisis. The town had been made the rendezvous point for the Royalist rebels from Essex and neighbouring Herefordshire. Prominent among them was Sir Charles Lucas, the Cavalier younger brother of the controversial Colchester monarchist Sir John Lucas. Uncharacteristically Sir John had disappeared to London at the first sign of trouble and took no part in the drama which followed. They were joined by Lord Capel and Sir George Lisle, bringing a contingent from Herefordshire. Meanwhile, the Essex-trained bands in the south of the county had also declared for the King. When they heard of the Kent debacle they took the county committee hostage and prepared to welcome the retreating army. But, despite this appearance of solidarity, the defeat at Maidstone had badly rattled many in their ranks. At a council of war some were for throwing down their arms immediately. Many actually quit and offered their allegiance to Parliament. Lucas, though, typically rose to the occasion.

Sir Charles was a total professional, a real member of the 'rough soldiery', trained in the slaughter of the continental wars. His sister Margaret said that he hated music and dancing, classifying it as 'too effeminate for masculine spirits'. The Earl of Clarendon, the Royalist historian of the Civil War and a leading actor in it, described him as 'of a nature scarce to be lived with; of no good understanding, of a rough and proud humour, and very morose in conversation'. But here he was the man for the occasion, having served the King with distinction in the First Civil War. He rallied the troops with a stirring cry to arms; they were not alone he said; Norfolk and Suffolk were ready to rise with them; the King had already escaped from the Isle of Wight and, as he spoke, was on a ship in the Thames, waiting to come ashore in triumph; Dover Castle had been captured; thus he, 'by lies and tricks seduced the people'. He then led them off, taking some of the county committee with them as a bargaining counter, towards his home town of Colchester. Parliamentary propaganda, afterwards, blamed him for the ensuing disaster:

> Sir Charles Lucas was conceived, and too true, to be the cause of the ruin of the place, his interest in the town drawing the army

> thither. He was the head of all those that did rise in this county and so brought the odium of the country upon him.

In the mind of Lucas, and the other rebel strategists, was the nebulous idea of marching north to meet the invading Scots, raising rebellion and recruiting an ever-expanding army on the way.

This was certainly the cause of deep concern for the cautious Colonel Whalley, the man detailed by Fairfax to shadow the rebels over from Kent. Whalley reported back:

> The enemy hath quit Chelmsford ... where as soon as he came he had 500 arms besides ordnance, without resistance. We marched close in the rear of him, but he doth so overpower us with foot that we cannot engage him but to the hazard of the brigade.

Whalley was able to tell Fairfax that at least Sir Thomas Honywood had been able to maintain the loyalty of the 1,200 trained bands in the north of Essex and he was joining him. But he urged his commander-in-chief:

> It behoves you to hasten all the foot up you can and to come yourself, otherwise the enemy will be suddenly formed into a considerable army and will engage us.

This was followed up the next day with a further alarming dispatch:

> Our friends report the enemy to be 3,000 horses and foot and like a snowball increasing. My Lord I desire to know which way and when your lordship comes.

Then later the same day: 'We desire your excellency should expedite your march the longer they are suffered the more numerous they grow'. Fairfax needed no such prompting. He had made a hasty, if rather shaky, crossing of the Thames between Gravesend and Tilbury and was on the way.

THE ASSAULT

The burghers of Colchester had been anxiously watching developments and on 4 June an anonymous diarist recorded, in his detailed chronicle of the entire siege:

> we were alarmed in the town that the Lord Goring [Earl of Norwich], the Lord Capel and a body of the loyal party who had been in arms in Kent ... had given General Fairfax the slip and, having passed the Thames at Greenwich, were advancing this way.'

Four days later the Colchester diarist noted 'they were advanced to Chelmsford'. On 9 June an advance party of Royalist cavalry arrived at Colchester and set about enlisting volunteers. Many of the town's weavers 'and such like people wanting employment listed, so they completed Sir Charles Lucas' Regiment, which was but thin, to 800 men'. By the following day it was obvious that a race was on between the two armies to reach Colchester first. The Royalists won, arriving with an estimated 5,600 horse and foot, but even then the more optimistic hoped that they would quickly move on. Indeed Matthew Carter, their Quartermaster General, said later that 'it was our first intentions only to quarter at Colchester for a night or two'. As ill fortune would have it, Fairfax and the main body of his troops were hot on their heels and on 12 June the Earl of Norwich euphemistically 'let the town know that he would take them [Colchester] into his majesty's protection and he would fight the enemy in that situation'.

The Royalist historian Clarendon, who later became Charles II's chief minister, observed that Colchester 'was not glad of their company'. Sir Charles Lucas, and a group of cavalrymen, hearing that his home town 'stood on their guard [and] would not receive them in arms put spurs to their horses and galloped [there] at full speed'. They found the gates shut and sixty horsemen drawn up to oppose them. One charge only, in which one of the defenders was shot dead, was all it took to scatter them and end all opposition to the Royalist take-over. The townspeople 'perceiving the body of the army coming ... sent out to treat with him [Lucas] and upon his engagement that the town should not be plundered the gates were opened'.

By the night of 12 June Fairfax, with an advance detachment of 1,000 horse, arrived at the village of Lexden, little more than a mile from the town walls. It was from that direction that the New Model Army threw itself into action at noon the following day, hoping to repeat the quick success of their assault on Maidstone. Matthew Carter, the Royalist Quartermaster, wrote an account of the siege shortly afterwards: 'the dispute grew close and very hot', he said and so fierce was the initial thrust that the Royalists were forced into an orderly retreat which 'gave encouragement to the enemy to prosecute their charge upon us, thinking themselves more than half victors

15 Junii, 1648.

The Particulars of the

FIGHT

AT

COLCHESTER

(Sent in a Letter to the Honorable *William Lenthal* Eſq; Speaker of the Honorable Houſe of Commons) was read in the houſe of Commons:

In which Letter it appears,

The Town is beſieged, and Five hundred of the Enemies were taken Priſoners, and Six hundred left the Town, Sixty that were killed buried in one Churchyard, beſides what was ſlain in the other part of the Town, Sir *William Campion* ſlain, One Knight more, Col: *Cook*, Major *Eyres*, Two other Majors, and other Officers, *Merſey* Fort taken, with two Culverins, two Sakers, and one Drake, and Col: *Steward*, Col: *Thornton* and Sir *Bar. Scudamore* taken raiſing forces near *Newmarket*.

ORdered by the Commons aſſembled in Parliament, That this Letter *be forthwith printed and publiſhed.* H: Elſynge, Cler. Parl. D. Com.

London, Printed for *Edward Huſband*, Printer to the Honorable Houſe of Commons. *June* 17. 1648.

12. Reports of the first battle at Colchester soon reached the streets of London, less than two days' march away. The future of Parliamentary government, it was thought, hung on the result. Unlike the attack on Maidstone, in Kent, the initial assault on the town failed to dislodge the rebels and a long siege ensued. (Essex County Council)

13. The site of the old Head Gate at Colchester as it looks today: here the Parliamentary forces managed briefly to fight their way in before being expelled again. Lord Capel just managed to secure the gate against further attack by jamming it shut with his swagger stick.

already'. But the withdrawal was 'as much out of policy as out of danger', drawing the Parliamentarians 'pelmel with the rest' through the narrow Head Gate and into Head Street. But having entered town they were surprised by Royalist detachments, waiting to ambush them from the side alleys and from the High Street, 'and most of them that had so rashly entered were cut to pieces'. The attackers were pushed back: 'The Lord Capel charged at the Head Gate, where the enemy was most pressing with a pike, till the gate could be shut'. He finally managed to secure it with his swagger stick. Quartermaster General Carter, in his version of events, written four years later, said: 'I never saw any men fight with more gallant resolution and courage; honourable lords and gentlemen ... ran the hazard of the private soldier'. He estimated that some 700 army troops were killed, including 'Colonel Needham and other prime officers', while 130 were taken prisoner. Before retreating the New Model Army set fire to some houses near the Head Gate hoping, said Carter, that the flames would be fanned by the wind and 'might burn the whole town'. In what was to be the first of many allegations of war crimes Carter maintained that in suburbs the next morning, 'scarce a house was unplundered ... and many poor men dead in their houses and the women and children fled'.

Having been denied a swift, Maidstone-style victory, Fairfax was forced to rethink his tactics. His army, smaller than the Royalists', numbering only about 4,000 and already badly mauled, withdrew to Lexden and proceeded to dig in. They 'cast up a fort upon the highway to secure the headquarters'; all roads in and out of Colchester were barricaded to prevent aid arriving from London and the escape of the garrison northwards towards Cambridgeshire. His troops were ordered to dig in immediately: 'every night [they] broke up fresh ground in several places running their line by degrees from one redoubt and fort to another'. It was the beginning of one of the most extensive complex of trenches and earthworks ever to be strung around a besieged town in England, with ten forts and four redoubts – a system designed to completely isolate the place, known to military engineers as circumvallation. 'They intended to plant themselves before us', said Carter, 'for a longer continuance than before we had imagined and block us up'. Observers concluded,

> that the Lord Fairfax, finding the garrison strong and resolute, and that he was in no condition to reduce them by force at least not without the loss of much blood, had resolved to reduce them by hunger.

Strategic considerations dominated the mind of Thomas Fairfax. One false move could release this entrapped, but still powerful Royalist army. They were within two days march of the country's capital and capable of reversing all his previous victories with disastrous results for Parliament. Within Colchester a diarist kept a daily account of developments: 'Their troops [are] also wanted to oppose several other parties who had in several parts of the kingdom taken arms for the King's cause'. The Lord General[1] would need all his vaunted military cunning to stay ahead in this game.

3

SINNING AGAINST SO MUCH LIGHT

Thomas Fairfax knew that he would need many more men to plug the gaps in his lines, seal off Colchester from the outside world and starve it into submission. Every recruit he could get would be valuable. Already 'divers gentlemen, with some assistance of men and arms, found means to get into the town' and there was a pool of similarly enthusiastic volunteers forming, especially in London where many apprentices, always a politically volatile lot, wanted to join the rebels. They protested at what they considered the city's spineless attitude towards the Royalist cause and the beleaguered of Colchester periodically boosted their morale by telling themselves that more apprentices were on the way. Just before the siege some fifty gentlemen rendezvoused in Hyde Park and forced their way through a Parliamentary force at Epping to join the rebels massing at Brentwood. Some merchants in the capital undertook to pay and equip anyone who wanted to fight in Essex and several hundred Londoners were among the prisoners who finally surrendered at Colchester.

While the Parliamentary fortifications – the leaguer as they became known collectively – were new and vulnerable to penetration the Royalist cavalry made repeated sallies out of the town and into the surrounding

14. Sir Thomas Honywood: he managed to swing the north Essex militias behind Parliament at the vital moment. Without the support of the locally trained militias, the trained bands as they were known, Fairfax would never have been able to isolate Colchester and starve it into submission. (Essex County Council)

countryside in search of provisions and recruits. On 21 June parties of horse and foot:

> were commanded to go into the Hundred of Tendring, for the bringing in of provisions, which returned the following day with a hundred sheep and fifty oxen and in such like manner provisions were brought to the public store house every night.

At about the same time, hearing that the surrounding countryside was in rebellion, a strike force from the garrison was sent out in support. But little came of the it: the rising in Linton, in the neighbouring county of Cambridgeshire, was rapidly dealt with by Parliamentary troops. According to Quartermaster General Carter, the enterprise was bedevilled by treachery: one of the rebels turned informer 'in order to ingratiate himself with the prevailing power'. Such treachery, he considered an 'epidemical disease in the kingdom'. The Colchester party remained at large for a week before returning 'safe with what men they had raised'. They crept back in through the positions occupied by infantry units from Suffolk 'encamped betwixt them and the town'. Agents were also sent out to recruit in Norfolk, Suffolk and Cambridgeshire, but they found their clandestine movements severely restricted: 'for them there was no passage left open' after the army had 'broken up the bridges' in many places.

These comings and goings, said Carter, 'much incensed with anger' the people in the Parliamentary leaguer, 'that they should suffer us to march through their quarters'. Allowing the enemy to continue these usually nocturnal wanderings behind the lines was also a very dangerous and terrifying business: the intruders had a habit of picking off any Parliamentary troops 'they found straggling from their posts, and by this means killed a great many'. Carter said that 'though we gave them no field-battle, yet we suffered them not to lie idle [by] constantly fighting in one place or other, both night and day'. But as the noose around the town was inexorably drawn tighter, this situation did not last. 'After that time', he recalled, 'we never obtained the like opportunity, the enemy drawing immediately near upon us, confining us within narrow bounds'.

Fairfax 'finding that he was not able to carry the town by storm sent to London and Suffolk for more forces'. He also demanded and got 'forty pieces of cannon from the Tower [of London]'. The locally trained bands were also ordered 'to be raised and posted on the roads to prevent succour'. Fortunately for the General (as we have seen) Sir Thomas Honywood and his 1,200 militiamen from north Essex and Suffolk stayed loyal to Parliament and proved to be vital in solving his pressing manpower problems. After it was all over Fairfax, in his report to Parliament, made a point of praising their dogged part in the final victory:

> The officers and soldiers of Essex and Suffolk (who in this time of dangerous defection, have adhered constantly to yours and the kingdom's interest) for their faithful demeanour and patient endurance in the hardships of this service, are not to be forgotten.

Fairfax went out of his way not to offend the local troops, so important was their cooperation: in mid-July he commuted a death sentence on one of the local officers, Captain Vesey, for 'practising and entertaining intelligence with the enemy and having communications with them without my directions.' He exercised his clemency after a plea for mercy was received from the Essex-trained bands. They believed that Vesey had committed his 'disservice' out of nothing more than 'slavish fear, of being a prisoner of the enemy,' and Fairfax felt he had no political option but to agree to mercy. This war, as never before, was all about competing ideologies; loyalty was a virtue to be carefully cultivated.

TRENCH WARFARE

The suffering of the soldiers both in the trenches and on the ramparts at Colchester was made worse by the appalling weather. The summer of 1648 was cold and incessantly wet, the latest in a long series of bad summers which had created widespread harvest failure, shortages and suffering. Once again crops lay rotting in sodden fields; the trenches around Colchester regularly filled with water; the River Colne, was brim full, making the fords across it useless for much of the time; most military movements were restricted to the few contested bridges. The Royalist newspaper *Mercurius Elencticus* reported that the 'loggerheads' of Parliament had to 'stand up to their knees in dirt, and look like so many drowned rats for four to six hours together'. Carter noted that a steady stream of Parliamentary troops deserted because of the conditions:

> through the severity of the weather divers came into town, three or four in a day and often more [with] others stealing away to their

> own habitations the countrymen [particularly] began to be displeased with the service and thought it hard duty to lie so long in the trenches and were glad to entertain all comers who would perform their duty for them.

Those who could afford it were prepared to pay surrogates ten shillings a week 'constant pay' to stand in for them. Many men 'came from London and other places' to take advantage of the offers.

Sieges, by their very nature, were fraught with potentially fatal consequences not only for the beleaguered, but also for those blockading them. Disease, the bane of armies for centuries – it killed many more men than battle – was just as likely to strike at them as at the garrison inside. Colonel Henry Ireton, Cromwell's son-in-law and the man who was to play such a controversial role in the drama which ended the siege of Colchester, was destined, a couple of years later, to fall victim to an epidemic which raged through his lines during the siege of Limerick in the west of Ireland. Newspaper reports from outside Colchester talked of sickness spreading through the leaguer, of 'agues and sickness ... which makes them drop very fast'. Carter maintained that 'the tediousness of the service weakens them by hard duty, constant action and unseasonal lying in the field in respect of the weather'. He took heart from the many 'gallant examples' in history where it was the besieged, not the besiegers, who eventually had won the war of attrition, citing people like Julius Caesar and the contemporary Prince of Orange in his struggle against the Spanish in the Netherlands. Victory could well come to the one who was able to stick it out the longest. Hostile newspapers began to speculate that, rather than trapping the Royalist force inside Colchester, Fairfax was himself the prisoner, unable to move while the Cavaliers there continued to menace the capital. They also maintained that the morale of his men was fast crumbling. The 'Saints' of the New Model Army, stated one, were 'no longer worthy of the name of an army' and 'King Tom [Fairfax]' had already 'fastened his own neck in a noose now no physician can cure him of his gout, but the hangman'.

The Royalists, bottled up inside the inadequate defences of Colchester, had perforce to play a waiting game. They too were anxious to avoid 'the hazard of an immediate ruin' by risking everything in one pitched battle. The decision made long-term strategic sense. Carter explained:

> We had hopes of speedy relief, both from the Scots and divers other places who were at the same time in action. Besides it was judged the greatest piece of policy to keep the enemy in lingering action

15. Parts of Colchester's ancient walls, like this bastion built originally by the Romans in Priory Street, were hastily incorporated into the garrison's defensive system. The large gaps that remained were filled by earthworks and make-shift barricades. The Royalists never intended to make a stand in such a difficult place to defend.

> to give a remora to their designs and ruin them by long delays.

If the New Model Army was forced to remain at Colchester their lethal fire power could not be brought to bear elsewhere. This would give:

> an opportunity to others who were in action to work their designs without interruption. It was no rash or fond supposition to think that we could hold what we had till the rest of the kingdom should rise, we should then do as good service as the immediate victory. We supposed we might possibly hold out for a month and were resolved upon it.

16. The Hythe, Colchester's riverside dock area, pictured in the eighteenth century: Fairfax made a rare tactical blunder when he allowed the Royalists to retain control of the docks just long enough to drain them of all their precious stores. Without these provisions it is unlikely that the siege could have lasted beyond ten days. (Essex County Council)

The Quartermaster General thought that this should give the Scots Engagers ample time to 'march quietly into the kingdom'. In the end their resistance lasted for a total of seventy-five ghastly days, as they watched one promise of relief after another founder before reaching them.

The garrison quickly pitched into the job of making the town a defensible proposition, 'strengthening the walls and fortifying those places where no wall was by casting up ramparts ... as a great part of the town required'. Outside the New Model Army were feverishly employed with pick and shovel:

> busy running their trenches ... and casting up forts and batteries against us, and we as diligent and laborious within ... not without necessity, the town being in all places very weak.

Private stores of food were confiscated where they could be found and impounded for the common good, but it amounted to a very meagre haul with which to feed more than 5,000 troops and a population that in normal times amounted to twice that number. But here the garrison had a stroke of good fortune.

The New Model Army, while consolidating its position after its initial attack was repulsed, had failed to realise the importance of the Hythe, Colchester's usually booming port, which lay slightly down river. Although it had been successfully closed to navigation, there remained on the dockside:

> many private stores of corn and wine of all sorts, with much salt, some fish and a good quantity of powder, the want whereof would suddenly have thrown us into absolute ruin, having much exhausted our magazine by the last day's business ... At the Hythe we found greater assistance than indeed we could have hoped for, which was conveyed into the town with expedition and secrecy, the enemy being so favourable as not to endeavour to cut us off from that place.

According to Carter this 'they might easily have done had they known what we were doing'. In no time at all the Royalists had 'almost drained the honey from the comb' – a providence 'almost as great as that of the Israelites in the wilderness'. He was confident that without the supplies of food and gunpowder at the Hythe 'we would not have kept possession of the town for ten days, for there lay the greatest part of our provision by which we afterwards subsisted'. He was in no doubt that Fairfax had made an elementary tactical blunder in not 'surprising the place in due time ... With much ease they might have taken it from us, for it lay so open for them to seize'.

Before Parliamentary forces put a stop to any relief reaching Colchester from the sea, two ships did manage to get through bringing food, corn and fifty-six rebels 'from the shore of Kent'. The ships 'were unloaded the same night into some hoys which brought it up to the Hythe', but the next day Parliamentary vessels from Harwich intercepted the ships 'in the mouth of the river'. It was the one and only attempt to run the blockade. Very early on the army had taken over the fort on the tip of Mersea Island, some six miles down river, which dominated the approaches to the Colne 'so that no boat could stir'. Its isolated position, so far from town, made it indefensible to the garrison, although on 20 June 300 men were sent out to make 'a show of attacking' it, while they rounded up 'a good number of cattle' and drove them back, together with 'five wagons laden with corn'. These supplies, however, were 'the last they could bring in that way, the lines being soon finished on that side'. Meanwhile the garrison were establishing their own front-line, just beyond the town wall, 'without the East Bridge and without the North Gate and Bridge and so plant more cannon upon the works'. At the same time the garrison still ventured out to harry the army engineers busy throwing up siegeworks to the south.

On 20 June Fairfax made his first offer of 'honourable conditions for surrender'. They included: 'Allowing all the gentlemen their lives and arms, exemption from plunder and passes if they desired to go beyond the sea'. The rank and file were to be pardoned and allowed 'to go peaceably to their own dwellings'. However, Fairfax made a point of declaring Sir Charles Lucas a special case. For him there would be no mercy because Fairfax alleged that the notorious Cavalier had broken his parole, previously given to him personally after he had surrendered to him at the battle of Marston

17. These old earthworks on Mersea Island are all that remain of the fort which guarded the approaches to the River Colne. The garrison was forced to abandon it to the army because it lay so far out of town, with the result that Colchester was closed to any relief from the sea.

COLCHESTERS 16

TEARES:

Affecting and Afflicting

CITY and COVNTRY;

DROPPING

From the ſad face of a new Warr, threatning to bury in her own Aſhes that wofull TOWN.

Faithfully collected, drawn out into a moderate Relation and Debate, humbly preſented to all Free-born *Engliſhmen*;

By ſeverall perſons of Quality.

Who much doubted and deſired to ſee the Truth in the miſt of various relations obſcuring the ſame, but now convinced by their own eyes, doe conceive themſelves bound to give out this brief Narrative, to ſatisfie all unprepoſſeſſed civil and moderate men, and good Chriſtians, who truly love Jeſus Chriſt, their King, City, and Countrey, and ſincerely deſire the ſettlement of *Peace and Truth.*

July 31

Have pity upon me, have pity upon me, O ye my friends; for the hand of the Lord hath touched me, Job 19. 21.

Is it nothing to you, all ye that paſs by? Behold and ſee, if there be any ſorrow like to my ſorrow which is done unto me, wherewith the Lord hath afflicted me, in the day of his fierce anger, Lament. 1. 12.

London, Printed for *John Bellamy* at the three Golden Lions, in Cornhill, near the Royall Exchange, 1648.

18. Parliamentary pamphlets like *Colchester Teares* had little sympathy for the dreadful plight of the civilians trapped in the beleaguered town. They were merely viewed as 'sad' examples of what happened when such communities 'traded with Cavaliers'.
(Essex County Council)

Moor in July 1644. According to Fairfax, by 'appearing in arms' again Lucas had 'forfeited his honour and faith and was not capable of command or trust in martial affairs'. Lucas denied the slur and the dispute later led to accusations that Fairfax had him shot as part of a squalid vendetta against the Royalist hero.

Norwich reportedly 'laughed at' Fairfax's offer, whereupon the General instantly withdrew the guarantee of quarter to the officers and told the troops that if they wanted to throw down their arms and desert they would have 'free leave to pass through their camp and go wherever they pleased without molestation'. Sure enough some of the men 'foreseeing the great hardships they were like to suffer, began to slip away' and Norwich threatened the death penalty for anyone who was caught trying. Twenty-four-hour patrols had to be introduced to hold the line 'notwithstanding which many of them got away'. By the beginning of July a form of conscription was being introduced among the civilians of Colchester with 'a proclamation calling for all townsmen as could serve upon the line ... to enlist themselves'. Everyone else was ordered to deliver any arms and ammunition they still possessed to the armory 'on pain of death'. Internal security was becoming a problem.

Nevertheless, in the midst of all this martial activity there was a brief and surreal flash of normality when the town's weavers petitioned Fairfax, across the lines, to be allowed to 'carry on their trade' as if nothing was happening. The bemused General observed that 'to desire free trade from a town besieged was never heard of'. And anyway, he told them, he could not entertain such a request from them: it would have to come from 'those who pretend the chief command there'. If they really wanted to send out the cloth he would undertake to sell it at a special market set up on Lexden Heath, but naturally nothing came of this suggestion. The weavers may have, in the past, shown admirable loyalty to the Parliamentary cause and the reformed religion, but all this had been squandered when they opened the town gates and let the Royalists in. Parliamentary propagandists had little sympathy for the plight of those penned in at Colchester. One pamphlet, entitled *Colchester Teares* thought that their situation should serve as an example to all those who were seduced from the godly path by the lure of mammon. 'We humbly hope and pray that all moderate men will a little look and by the sad example of mournful and much lamented Colchester, take a warning in time'. Their 'desolate' state was their own fault 'since they traded with cavaliers and admitted them freely to their town'. None of the papers suggested just how these unarmed civilians were supposed to have defended themselves against an approaching army of desperate men in full retreat. It was a significant measure of how intolerant and uncompromising the combatants had become by the summer of 1648. Their quarrel now involved deep convictions and dark allegations of treachery and betrayal.

SAINTS AND SINNERS

For the radical 'Saints' of the godly New Model Army, the King had put himself beyond negotiation, preferring labyrinthine intrigues to an honest attempt at settlement. His Engagement with the Scots, inviting aid from what the vast majority of Englishmen still considered to be a foreign invader amounted to a final act of treason against his own people. It had been proved long ago that Charles was willing to hire help from any foreign quarter, including the barbarian Irish, to re-establish his reign. Cromwell wrote that this Second Civil War was:

> a more prodigious treason than any that had been perpetrated before, because the former quarrel [the First Civil War] was that Englishmen might rule over one another; this war is to vassalise us to a foreign nation.

For most Parliamentarians, and certainly for the troops of the undefeated New Model Army, their first victory over the King was a sure sign that their cause, in the eyes of God, was a just one. Anyone, therefore, trying to reverse the result of this divine decision, was guilty of a much more serious offence, that of sacrilege – of challenging the will of the Almighty. As Cromwell put it: 'it is a repetition of the same offence against all the witnesses that God has borne, by making and abetting a second war'. What made this crime all the worse, and certainly more unnerving for a Parliament desperately hanging onto power, was that some of its most reliable but politically moderate old soldiers from the first war were going over to the other side. For the hard-liners this was treason compounded; it was unforgivable. The rebellion, which was reducing South Wales to turmoil, was being conducted by just such men. 'They have sinned against so much light', said Cromwell, 'and against so many evidences of divine presence, going along with and prospering a righteous cause'. At the beginning of May he was marching west, taking nearly half the New Model Army with him, to deal with them.

In South Wales, the rumbustious Colonel John Poyer, as we have already seen, had set rebellion in motion by taking over Pembroke Castle and now the rebels added a more prestigious name to their number – Major-General Rowland Laugharne. His defection came as a great shock to Parliament. He was their most distinguished local commander and they had every reason to be grateful to him when, the previous year, he had promptly and efficiently put down a Royalist rebellion in his native Glamorgan. But even so many government supporters in South Wales distrusted him for protecting Royalist delinquents. The High Sheriff of Pembrokeshire complained: 'there is not scarce a royal malignant in this county that wants [lacks] his protection'. Laugharne was indeed a political moderate, extremely reluctant after the war to have his local military command absorbed into the New Model Army or even to accept the overall authority of Fairfax as commander-in-chief. He backed his men when they complained of being the most heavily in arrears with their pay of any Parliamentary force. Many who were demobilised went off immediately to join Colonel Poyer. When, on 4 April, two more companies of Laugharne's horse rode off to join Poyer, Parliament considered it was time to act and sent a strong force under

Colonel Horton to discipline their reluctant Major-General. Laugharne protested to Parliament: 'I was confident my past service had merited much better of you'. When Laugharne eventually faced Horton's superior numbers at St Fagan's, near Cardiff, on 8 May his defeat was overwhelming. However, he managed to escape from the battlefield and made his way to Pembroke where he joined Poyer himself. They were a badly matched pair from the start and fiery arguments soon followed. At one stage it was reported that Laugharne came at Poyer with a drawn sword, threatening to run him through. Fate, however, linked this odd couple inextricably together and soon they would face the righteous wrath of Oliver Cromwell.

There were smaller risings in various parts of the country, like the one at Linton, not far from Colchester. Other bushfires broke out in Nottinghamshire, Lincolnshire, Huntingdon, Rutland, Leicestershire, Hertfordshire, Sussex, Dorset, Hampshire, Surrey, Worcestershire and Warwickshire. They were all quickly dealt with, but they badly rattled members of the Derby House Committee responsible for scrambling the national defences to meet the multiple challenges. Most rebellions were organised by the local gentry; the only one raised by aristocrats took place at Kingston-upon-Thames, but for all that it was farcical affair. The prime mover was the Earl of Holland, the brother of the Lord Admiral Warwick. He was a courtier, not a soldier – 'a man fitter for a show than a field' – a favourite of the exiled Queen Henrietta Maria. At the outbreak of the war in 1642 he was a supporter of Parliament, albeit one in favour of sweeping concessions to the King. But he rapidly turned into a serial defector: when the fortunes of Parliament reached their lowest point in 1643 he absconded to join Charles at Oxford, but even royal service at the siege of Gloucester and at the first battle of Newbury failed to restore him to the confidence of the court. In October he returned to Westminster, with two other noble defectors, to be greeted there by 'silent contempt', brief imprisonment and the partial sequestration of his property. His influence in the affairs of the nation had been forever destroyed and here could be found the seeds of the rebellion which flourished at the beginning of July. His brother encouraged him saying that 'the Scots should not do all the work' in restoring the King.

He was joined by the Duke of Buckingham and the Earl of Peterborough with the object of raising the southern counties against Parliament, followed by the capital itself. The duke bowed to pressure from the exiled queen and her court in France and allowed the incompetent Holland to take command. There followed a series of pointless manoeuvres in Surrey and then military disaster at Kingston-upon-Thames, in which the duke's brother was killed. The whole expedition then drifted north with the grandiose intention of relieving Colchester. The whole affair reached its ludicrous denouement at St Neots in Huntingdonshire. The exhausted remnants arrived 'weary and shaken in their joints'. The earl himself looked as though 'he had a better will to his bed than his horse'. They were completely surprised by Colonel Scroope and his detachment from the New Model Army at Colchester. The Duke of Buckingham and the Earl of Peterborough succeeded in getting away and eventually escaped abroad, but Holland was captured and imprisoned at Warwick Castle before being tried by a special high court in February 1649 and beheaded.

For a brief moment these ultimately doomed efforts to raise the country for the King, served to buoy up the waning morale of those trapped behind the walls of Colchester. So too did the unpredictable antics of the naval vessels which had mutinied against Parliament and were now under the command of the eighteen-year-old Prince of Wales. He found himself in control of a sizeable section of the navy and able to call on the logistical backing of both the Dutch and the French for such things as victuals and port facilities. It was broadly rumoured that he planned to 'strike again at some other place' and most predictions favoured Essex as the target, with the relief of Colchester as the major objective, 'to let those birds at liberty, which he esteems to be the only instrument to advance his father's cause'. The pro-Royalist *Mercurius Bellicus* reported that he had with him 6,000 'superior' men and 'intends shortly to visit his Lameship [the gouty Fairfax] at push of pike. He hath with him the flower of chivalry, consisting of English and French'. This sort of propaganda played on Parliament's paranoid obsession with foreign invasion. The newspaper also added: 'Nor hath he want of money [because] being arrived he knows there is no lack of gold in London'. This was aimed directly at the money-bags of the City: if they knew what was good for them, they would invest in a Royalist victory voluntarily and invest soon, before the King arrived to take the money off them by force. The piratical presence of the Prince's navy, prowling the coast, was also used as a weapon to coerce the merchants of the City, ever worried by the effect of the war on their trading profits. Privateering, the licensed piracy of Parliamentary shipping in the Channel and the North Sea, was considered a legitimate weapon of commercial warfare. The Royalist paper, the *Parliament Kite*, warned the merchants that they must 'speedily advance to him [the Prince of Wales] the sum of £20,000, else he will pay himself twice so much upon the sea'. If things went on the way they were 'trading ere long in the City will be only between the Independents and the

19. Charles, Prince of Wales: the Prince, the future Charles II, was eighteen when he escaped abroad and eventually took command of the ships of the Royal Navy which mutinied against Parliament. It was feared that he would use this fleet to back a foreign invasion on behalf of his imprisoned father and land reinforcements on the East Anglian coast to relieve Colchester and march on London.

Brothers of the Presbytery'. But as the days of siege at Colchester dragged into weeks the promise of seaborne relief slowly faded.

It was from the north that Colchester's real hope of salvation lay. There an invading Scots army was supposed, with all possible speed, to march south on London to place the King back on his throne, relieving them on the way. The long-expected invasion finally got under way on 8 July, but here, as elsewhere, things were not proceeding according to plan – the Scots cavalry were hopelessly late in riding to the rescue.

INVASION

When Charles I signed the secret Engagement with the Scots back in January it was envisioned that their invasion army would become the lynchpin of his plan to regain power. However, both signatories had reckoned without the volatile changes in the political climate which were to take place north of the border. The Engagement came about in the first place because of a deep division in the Scottish Covenanting party. It was promoted by the more conservative elements and represented an effort by the Scots nobility and moderate gentry of the Covenant to snatch back control from the radical and godly party, which had the backing of the extremists of the Kirk. The Engagers, playing on old prejudices, argued, sometimes very effectively, that by allying with the King they could use him against the perceived intentions of Westminster to turn Scotland into 'an English Province'. With some skilful political manoeuvring they were able to gain the upper hand in the Scottish Parliament and push through plans to raise the necessary men to invade England once again, the third time in eight years. The Kirk, however, continued its virulent opposition and fought the recruiting drive tooth and nail. As a result it took an inordinate length of time, much too long as it later transpired, to raise less than a third of the projected quota of troops. Not only were they unacceptably late and under-strength when they finally crossed the border on 8 July, but the pro-Royalist rebellions of their potential allies in England were rapidly running out of steam. The English rebels had been completely incapable of harnessing their cause to the strong anti-government feeling which had swept the country: vital coordination was non-existent. That the Scots were late, badly armed, woefully under-supplied and led by a set of quarrelling and inept generals did not help. Nor did the fact that south of the border they were almost universally distrusted and despised, even by the Royalists whose bacon they were supposed to be saving.

The Scots were viewed by most Englishmen as little more than barbarians, only marginally more civilised than the Irish. Their invasion of England, necessary to the Royal cause under the circumstances, would have to be tolerated, for the time being at least. But no Royalist could forget their intervention on the side of Parliament in the First Civil War and many, perhaps rightly, blamed their ultimate defeat in 1646 on that. As one of the Prince of Wales's close advisers put it: 'A pox on the Scots, they have done us more hurt than good, they are crafty rogues.' The necessity of a Scots intervention also stuck in the craw of the Royalist press. *Parliament's Vulture* commented on 22 June:

> 'Tis supposed that they [Scots] will prove honest contrary to nature. The truth is they had rather feed on good beef and bacon than on oat cakes and colworts and if England must be ransacked, robbed and ruined, the Scots can plead as much liberty as the Independents.

Many agreed that they would prefer to see the new allies 'steer some other course, and set sail for Geneva or Amsterdam [centres of radical Calvinism] where their faction will be welcomer than their persons'. But they were on their way and the spectre of an approaching host of some 15,000 men must have provoked feelings of panic and dread among the MPs at Westminster, whose hands were already full of trouble much closer to home, not two days march from the capital, in Essex.

Whatever the rest of their allies thought about the Scots, their imminent arrival now assumed monumental importance to the battered garrison in Colchester. On 10 July Lord Capel wrote to Sir Marmaduke Langdale, the commander of the Royalist rebels in the north, who had by then joined up with the Scottish troops. Capel optimistically believed that Langdale had already reached Lincoln on a triumphal march south and 'thought it fit to advertise you somewhat of our condition at Colchester'. Their horses needed fodder, but:

> neither the enemy nor we are idle, yet we conceive that our tying and obliging Fairfax to us is the best way of proceeding for his majesty's service, for the rest of the kingdom have more scope to act their parts by it.

A Royalist defeat at Colchester, said Capel, would 'let him [Fairfax] loose, which is the reason we hazard not more than needs must stand with our duty and honour'. Capel thought that to engage in an all out battle with Fairfax could prove 'a disaster', considering 'the advantage the enemy hath of us in numbers'. Capel went on:

> If this finds you according to our expectations near Cambridge Fairfax and his army will not nearer attend your coming, and you are at your election to march directly to us, or to go to London as shall be most requisite for the King's service.

And he added, rather wistfully: 'though we should be glad to have the advantage by your coming to us to be relieved'. Langdale, never left Lancashire and never got the letter; it was intercepted while being smuggled across the lines.

This was a time of maximum logistical stress for the New Model Army. The military rising dragged on in South Wales; the Scots, as feared, were finally on the way; a still dangerous Royalist force was being contained at Colchester, just two days' march from the capital, where increasing numbers of MPs were ready to cave in to the King and where powerful commercial interests were busy campaigning for his return. Things remained grim for a hopelessly divided government. But within a matter of days came the first signs of an upturn in their fortunes. Within twenty-four hours of Capel penning his note to Langdale the rebellion in South Wales finally collapsed with the surrender to Cromwell of Pembroke Castle.

On 14 June Cromwell had reported to Parliament that he did not think that the place would hold out for more than a fortnight, so low were they on supplies. But despite the feud between the unpredictable Poyer and the reluctant rebel Laugharne, and signs of serious mutiny within the garrison, they held out for almost a month more. Here too the defenders hung on hoping for Langdale to ride over the horizon to their rescue, but as time dragged by the Roundheads could hear, from their forward trenches, loud quarrels going on behind the castle walls. The rank and file were in a mutinous mood: 'Shall we be ruined for two or three men's pleasure', was the question they heard shouted, 'better that we should throw them over the walls'. Five weeks later scenes of uncanny similarity were to be repeated at Colchester. Finally the men threatened to cut Poyer's throat if he did not surrender within six days. He was left with no option. According to Fairfax Poyer, Laugharne and a third Welshman, Colonel Rice Powell, who had played a much more shady part in the whole episode, had 'betrayed the trust reposed in them to the sad engaging the kingdom again in blood and war'. Nonetheless, they managed to escape the summary fate of their comrades Lucas and Lisle at Colchester, and were spared an immediate firing squad. Later, though, they all faced capital charges at a court martial. In the end only one was required to face the execution squad, to provide the example, and they drew lots as to who it should be. Poyer lost.

WAITING FOR THE SCOTS

Cromwell was at last free to move his half of the New Model Army northwards, as fast as he dare march them, to deal with the Scots' challenge, leaving Fairfax to contain Colchester and the Home Counties. Royalist commentators claimed that Major-General John Lambert, who had been strong enough to contain the northern rebellion until the arrival of the Scots, had been sending 'many pitiful complaints' to Fairfax about the 'great danger

20. Major-General John Lambert: he commanded units of the New Model Army in the north. Lambert was ordered to wait for Oliver Cromwell to reinforce him before he tackled a Royalist rebellion there. Cromwell force-marched his army from Wales clear across England to meet the new dangers posed by an invading Scots army.

that he was in'. With the Scots now on English soil reinforcements were said to have been 'spared out his Excellency's [Fairfax's] army before Colchester [and] are now set forward towards Nottingham where they expect to find King Noll [Cromwell] himself in person'. For Cromwell it was a desperate march, but achieved with all his immense talent for logistical detail. The Parliamentary paper, the *Perfect Weekly Account,* told its readers that as his troops passed through Shropshire their boots began to wear out. 'Had the foot [soldiers] but whole shoes and stockings it would be great comfort to the wearied soldiers, and a special means to expedite their long march to Major-General Lambert'. Orders were sent ahead to the cobblers of Northampton and the stocking makers of Coventry to get to work on 1,500 pairs of footwear to be ready at Leicester where the army stopped briefly on 1 August to re-equip itself. Cromwell went on ahead, with his cavalry, taking with him only 3,000 of his best infantry, picking up local contingents along the way in Leicestershire, Nottinghamshire and Derbyshire. He took the long looping eastern route to collect badly needed supplies, but also to make sure that he met Lambert in Yorkshire before facing the invaders. Their combined forces would still only number half those of the enemy. Lambert was ordered to avoid any engagement before Cromwell's arrival and was forced to fight several tactical withdrawals as a result.

The Scots invasion put heart into many would-be rebels, although the government managed to snuff out a series of insurrections before they became established and foiled plots to seize both Portsmouth and Oxford. With the Prince of Wales loose on the high seas many coastal installations had been encouraged to back the Royalists. The governor of Scarborough Castle declared for the King and Deal, Walmer and Sandwich Castles in Kent, which protected the anchorage at the Downs, were still holding out against Parliament. More government troops were needed to retain control of large areas of the West Country, where Royalism continued to be rampant. There was further trouble brewing in north Wales – one of the reasons why the Scots commander, the Duke of Hamilton decided to take his army down the longer, westerly route south, through Lancashire, when he finally decided to stir himself and move. He had spent much of July in frustrating inaction, waiting for guns, supplies and reinforcements to catch up with him along the waterlogged roads and the swollen rivers of that cold and saturated summer. He was also bedevilled with endless divisions among his commanders, some of whom even refused to recognise his authority. It was a fatal delay, an ominous sign of things to come, but in Colchester Hamilton's army still represented fresh hope in their steadily tightening corner of this scattered national battlefield.

By the end of June Fairfax had succeeded in bringing up some heavier artillery to batter beleaguered Colchester. Royalist troops were driven from Grimston's house at the Maldon-Lexden road junction by the guns of Barksted's Fort and Parliament's gunners also shelled, for the first time, the tower of St Mary's at the Walls Church, which served as an important observation post for the garrison and where they had also installed one of their few heavy artillery pieces. From there they were able to shoot directly at several choice army targets with devastating effect. Although the barrage failed to silence the gun 'one of our best gunners of the garrison was killed with a cannon bullet'. The enemies' siegeworks were also inching nearer to the town all the time. The Colchester diarist wrote on 26 June that they had bridged the River Colne upstream, at Mile End, and built forts on each side, named after Colonel Ewers and Colonel Rainsborough, 'so that the town was entirely shut in on that side and the Royalists had no place to get out but East Bridge'. When, at the beginning of July, the army threatened to cut even that

21. The tower of St Mary's at the Walls (the old town wall can still be seen in front of the church) was an important observation post and gun platform for the garrison. Fire could be directed so accurately from it that it became a prime target for enemy gunners and the damage they caused can still be seen today.

route, the garrison reacted with a determined counter-attack, but one that was to demonstrate how weakened, by then, was their ability to hit back.

Carter reported that 'the enemy ... fell into East Street and seized the mill on the river'. It was decided to respond with 'a grand sally on that part of the town' led by Sir Charles Lucas and Sir George Lisle with 500 foot and 200 cavalry. But 'whilst the enemy's guard was placed on both sides of the street and a barricado across it' there was 'no other passage across the river than a foot bridge'. The men ran the gauntlet of fire as they raced in single file across it, took the barricade and threw the enemy guns into the river. They 'made good the charge until they cleared the whole street, which gave great alarm to their leaguer'. One party, carried by the momentum of their attack, raced on past the mill before they 'discovered they had spent all their ammunition'. The opposition was alerted to their plight when they overheard shouts for more powder and shot to be brought up, and instantly charged them from behind a hedge, killing most or taking them prisoner. The rest withdrew 'in very good order' back into town. Carter reported: 'In this action Sir George Lisle was once taken prisoner, but immediately rescued'. He reckoned that they lost a captain, a lieutenant and thirty men, but claimed the army suffered 200–300 dead, plus eighty taken prisoner. 'Though the saints of our time would make us believe they have found a way of fighting to kill thousands', he said, ''tis only tongue charms which guard their armies and not divine providence which conducts them to such miracles'. He also maintained that this 'grand sally' had resulted in many desertions in the leaguer. Whatever the truth of these optimistic claims it had shown up the garrison's worsening weakness – they were running out of ammunition and with the best fighting will in the world, they were lost without it. Carter admitted that: 'The next night the enemy strengthened their leaguer in that part of the town and possessed themselves of their former ground'.

Colchester's famous bullet-scarred Siege House still bears witness to the encounter, but it was lucky to survive because the army then set fire to many of the houses in that area so that they could not be used to cover a further such counter attack from town; they also tried to fire all the windmills 'thinking thereby to hinder us from grinding our corn'. But one of the bonuses the garrison found at the Hythe was a cache of several mill stones stored at the dockside, which they had the forethought to drag into town. With these, several horse-drawn mills were set up 'which proved very serviceable during the siege'. The army expended a great deal of ammunition on shelling the one remaining serviceable mill they could see, the

22. Direct evidence of the battles at Colchester can still be seen at the half-timbered Siege House, which stands on the other side of the bridge at the end of East Street. It was here that the garrison staged one of their biggest attacks in an effort to prevent the army closing in on the town.

23. and 24. The fury of the battle at East Street can be judged by the bullet holes which peppered the building.

Middle Mill at the river's edge on the northern side of town 'over against the Warren', but they did 'little damage'. They were unaware that there were now available other means of making flour. 'They thought', wrote Carter, 'if they disabled us from grinding corn for the soldiers, they would mutiny for want of bread'. But bread supplies had by now been made a priority under the 'diligent care' of Lord Loughborough, whose job it was to keep 'his strict eye over both mills and bakers'. Like the precious supplies of ammunition they had to be carefully husbanded – the siege was tightening daily.

On 2 July the Colchester diarist noted: 'The whole town was shut in at which the besiegers gave a general salvo from their cannon at all their forts'. But the Royalist command was determined to give the opposition a violent run for its money. They fired a return salvo and after dark crept out to attack, once again, Barkstead's Fort on the south side of the town, astride the Maldon Road. Fierce hand-to-hand fighting followed:

> with such fury that they twice entered the works sword in hand, killed most of the defendants and spoiled part of the fort's cast up [earthworks], but [with] fresh forces coming up they retired with little loss, bringing eight prisoners and having slain, as they reported, above one hundred.

The diary gloomily noted, however, that the news filtering into the Colchester from the outside world was beginning to sound more depressing:

> About this time we received by a spy the bad news of the defeating of the King's friends in almost all parts of England and particularly several parties which wished well to our gentlemen and intended to relieve them.

They also heard, via a Parliamentary defector, that what remained of the insurrection in Kent was dying fast. Walmer Castle, one of the main fortifications guarding the Downs, had surrendered to Parliament. But the Earl of Norwich, as commander-in-chief at Colchester, felt it was time to put on a brave face and on 12 July made an offer to the Parliamentary troops of the leaguer, which was also designed 'to be dispersed' further afield. 'Heaven seems pleased with our proceedings and earth conspires for our deliverance', he pronounced, before offering a general amnesty to all who crossed the lines and joined them. Considering the 'number of souls who have been

6. Julii, 1648.

From the

LEAGUER

A T

Colcheſter,

More certain News of the

F I G H T

on Wedneſday laſt;

A N D

Of their preſent condition.

P*Rinted by the Appointment of the Honorable Committee at* Derby-houſe.

G U A L T H E R F R O S T Secr'

London, Printed for *Edward Huſband*, Printer to the Honorable Houſe of Commons, *July* 8. 1648.

25. By 2 July Colchester had been completely 'shut in', but the Royalist command was still determined to carry the fight to the enemy. Reports like this appeared regularly in the press until, increasingly, the garrison were forced on to the defensive by their shortage of ammunition. (Essex County Council)

seduced by the imposture of pretended liberty' by Parliament, he said that 'whatever officer or soldiers now in arms against us shall, on or before 21 July repair to us, or join any part of our forces shall have his or their arrears of pay paid unto them'. They were also offered 'from his most sacred majesty an Act of Indemnity'. He also guaranteed that there would be 'no alteration in either Church or Commonwealth, but such as this present parliament hath declared'.

It was all bluster. By now both the garrison and the civilians packed into Colchester were feeling the very severe pinch of shortage. A month before, many of the quick thinking well-to-do had been able to flee in the narrow window of opportunity left open to them between sighting the Royalist vanguard and the arrival of the New Model Army, but a large number of the townspeople were 'very indigent and needy', hardly in a position 'to provide for themselves, nor had they scarcely been when the town was open'. Worsening relations between the garrison and these increasingly hostile citizens were soon to prove a cause of deep insecurity for the Royalist commanders.

4

THOSE MERCILESSE MECHANICKS

As July drew to its tortured close the siege of Colchester visibly tightened. The garrison's supplies of gunpowder were dwindling fast, limiting its scope for action and forcing it more and more on to the defensive: it had to be strictly rationed to the points on the perimeter most at risk. The cavalry too was being rapidly emasculated, the condition of their starving horses making them fit only for the table and some of them were barely good enough for that. With provisions failing 'the town now began to be greatly distressed'; the civilian population trapped inside 'were numerous [and] very uneasy'. They were, from the garrison's point of view, not only a liability, surplus to the war effort – so many non-combatant mouths to feed – but a brooding source of potential trouble. They were denied escape by Fairfax, who was well aware that a starving population, driven to desperation and riot, would soon become one of his greatest weapons in breaking the deadlock. Try as they might, even Colchester's normally influential civic leaders had failed to get exit visas from the Lord General for their families. The Parliament-inclined *Moderate* newspaper reported on 6 July:

26. An artist's impression of the lurid scene when many of the defenders at the Lucas family home were blown to pieces after the powder magazine at the Gate House was hit by an army grenade. The engagement was a significant set-back for the garrison. (Essex County Council)

> Yesterday, one mistress Burton and mistress Earns and other women, whose husbands are active in Colchester against the Army, came out, being fearful to stay in the town, but having not a general pass, were sent in again.

Follow-up stories in other publications suggested that the womenfolk finally succeeded in smuggling themselves out by boat. The wife of one 'well affected' town worthy also managed to complete the risky journey across the front-line. All the while military pressure on Colchester's defences was being stepped up.

On 23 July 'the enemy drew down on the Hythe'. The old port, now drained of its provisions and munitions, was no longer worth defending. 'Captain Horsmander ... no sooner saw the enemy, but he delivered up his guard without firing one musket though the place could have been maintained'. A tactical withdrawal into town was completed without too much trouble, but the squeeze from that quarter continued with 'the enemy drawing their line still nearer the Lord Lucas's house' – the old St John's Abbey. Under the cover of an old wall the army brought up some demi (light) cannons and began 'battering upon the Gate House (wherein was a guard of some one hundred musketeers) and reduced one side of it to the

27. The Abbey Gate was the scene of some fierce fighting as the Parliamentary leaguer tightened its grip on the town. Most of what we see today was rebuilt in the years after the war.

28. Some of the Abbey Gate remained intact, like this section of the vaulted ceiling and the damage caused by cannon and shot can still be seen.

ground'. The fighting continued at close quarters before the attackers managed to lob into the building 'two or three grenadoes at the same time'. The effect was devastating when they managed to hit the central magazine. The building was largely demolished in the huge explosion which followed and 'most of the gallant defenders buried in the ruins'. The survivors struggled from the 'stones and dust' but, unable to:

> stand the shock, betook themselves to their swords and the butt ends of their muskets, and fought very hard from one place to another till most of them got away, some out of the wicket of the gate and others out of the windows and broken places of the house. The officers also forced their liberty with the points of their swords and came all off safe.

It was a victory for the army, but one which 'they purchased with the loss of many a stout man'. Carter admitted only reluctantly that the action may have been 'of some advantage to them', but the Gate House was obviously an important link in the overall defences of the town, 'a very strong pass and always well guarded'. The anonymous author of the siege diary considered that its loss was 'a great blow for the Royalists'.

The New Model Army also took possession of the now-deserted Lucas mansion and despite the fact that it had been stripped of most of its valuables in the pre-war riots of 1642, proceeded to complete the job. Finding only a few sticks of furniture – they 'broke open the vault wherein the ancestors of Lord Lucas's family were usually interred, under pretence of searching for money'. They opened the lead coffins of Lady Lucas and Lady Killigrew:

> dismembered their trunks, throwing a leg in one corner of the vault and an arm in the other and were so impudent in this brutish act as to make away with the hair of those ladies' heads in their hats as a triumphant bravado in honour of their villainy.

The sacrilege sickened Carter: 'Is not that commonwealth happy which must receive a reformation of such Saints?'

An artillery duel developed around St Mary's at the Walls Church, a prime target for the army because of its importance as an observation post for the garrison. They kept:

> a sentinel continually there who discovered their [the army's] motion, both night and day, besides which [there was] made a platform in the frame of the bells and planted a brass saker [a small cannon] which, flanking their trenches, did them much injury.

The Royalist gunner who caused all the trouble became famous as a one-eyed man called Thompson. On 24 July the army opened up on the tower with two demi-cannons:

> They fired upwards of sixty shot at the steeple, but did very little damage ... A battery was raised against them from when we had not fired more than four times before one of their best cannoneers fell and with him six more; upon which, finding that place too warm for their continuance, they removed their guns from hence.

But the tower took another pounding the following day 'with their bigger pieces of battery', this time to greater effect: 'one side of which was some hours after beaten down.' Thompson was killed and his gun sent crashing

29. The damage caused by Parliamentary shelling is still evident at the tower of St Mary's at the Walls. The army gunners aimed to dislodge a Royalist cannon housed there. The artillery piece was nick-named Humpty Dumpty and local legend says that its destruction was the origin of the old nursery rhyme.

from its perch. Local folklore has it that the gun was called Humpty Dumpty, hence the nursery rhyme which says that: 'All the King's horses [the cavalry], and all the King's men [the infantry] / Couldn't put Humpty together again.'

The successful attack on the Lucas house, drew the siege trenches 'still more straight about us', while the shelling of St Mary's Church and general activity all along the siegeworks 'alarmed us round the line', especially as it coincided with an assault on Middle Mill, at the river's edge on the north side of Colchester 'over against Rye Gate'. Here, also on the night of 25 July, troops commanded by Colonel Rainsborough got 'over the river at a fordable place', despite the fact that it was in full spate due to the heavy rain, and 'fell upon them [the garrison] furiously obliging them to retreat into the town'. To Carter it looked like the opening sally of a full-scale effort to overrun Colchester, but 'a party in the town (chiefly gentlemen) marched down upon them with such resolution and spirit, that they were obliged to take to their legs and run away, first throwing down their arms'. In the panic of retreat 'many of them, mistaking the proper place to get [back] over the river, were drowned in their passage'. Carter was convinced that: 'This night the enemy intended to have stormed the town but, on meeting with this repulse, laid aside their design'. As a further precaution, trenches were dug behind the town walls to reinforce all the weak points on the western side, as the Colchester diarist put it: 'in case of storm they might meet a warm reception'. Norwich, also bothered now by increasingly accurate sniper fire, ordered the burning down of some suburban houses which lay too close to his positions for comfort, 'from whence their musketeers fired against the town'.

Carter grimly noted that continually,

> the enemy ... crept with their approaches nearer and nearer to us; yet many of their men paid dearly for their boldness. Though, by scarcity of ammunition, we could not make great sallies upon them, nor constantly fire from the line.

Nevertheless Carter said that smaller actions were fought 'almost every day' until the end of the siege and 'our shot so carefully disposed of, that many of them fell daily'. Carter observed that 'by this time our magazine began to be pretty near empty [and] all our flesh being spent'. The condition of the horses had 'also sunk' as they progressively became 'unfit for service'. Casualties were high among the men who were detailed to get forage for them: they were 'often killed when going out to cut and bring in grass for the horse some firing at the enemy while others cut the grass. All the thatch from the houses and boughs from the trees [had been] eaten up.'

At the next council of war it was decided that the cavalry mounts should be culled. 'The third part of every troop was drawn out to be killed', and orders went out to all officers of whatever rank to surrender their animals and make no attempts to 'conceal their horses'. As many of the slaughtered animals as possible were cured for storage, using up the meagre supplies of salt that remained, and the whole operation was turned into a macabre party with some of the carcasses 'immediately distributed to the men' who 'cheerfully fed upon them rather than deliver themselves up to the enemy upon base or dishonourable terms'. The smell of roasting drifted across the lines and the Parliamentarians were said to be 'greatly startled for before then they hoped and expected our daily submission to a treaty of surrender'. By the beginning of August Carter said that 'the greatest part of our horse had changed stables for slaughter-houses and their riders took up with foot arms'. The gentlemen were issued with halberds and the private troopers had to make do with hooks and sickles fitted to the end of long staves, 'which were very terrible for execution'. No man, he insisted, was 'idle for want of arms'.

A MISERABLE CONDITION

Conditions in Colchester at the end of July were deteriorating fast, which did not help the internal security situation. Carter alleged that there was a fifth column of 'poisonous incendiaries' at work within the town 'who had privately intruded themselves' and were now busy inflaming the local population. The Royalist press had already warned the garrison

> to be as vigilant as they are valiant and to have an eye behind them, for their enemies at Westminster are at no small charge in hiring eyes to overlook their actions and maintaining of knaves and rascals to betray their gallantry to ruin.

A month later, towards mid-July, the same paper, *Mercurius Melancholicus*, claimed that Fairfax had failed in an attempt to foment a civilian uprising 'by a cunning plot, which [was] discovered to Sir Charles Lucas by an alderman's wife'. According to the story, her husband was one of the principal conspirators, but her tip-off led to 'the birds [being] taken in their own nest' before the coup could take place. Carter certainly distrusted the townspeople, who had been far from enthusiastic about the arrival of the Cavaliers. 'The townspeople were always ready to second them', he said and exploit the mounting municipal discontent.

Units of the New Model Army, for instance, had made repeated attempts to burn the Middle Mill; it was an important strong point as well as being a source of flour, and had been saved once already by troops carrying water from the nearby river in their hats. By its destruction they hoped to create chronic food shortages. Already strict rationing had been introduced to eke out the supplies now coming from the horse-powered mills of the garrison, but the mayor, William Cooke, appeared to be incapable of imposing similar controls for the civilians 'who, by this time, began to be in want'. Carter was quick to read a malicious motive into this:

> whether out of rebellious wilfulness, or sottish simplicity I leave others to judge, [the Mayor] rather desired to hazard the starving of them [the population], thinking that by the violent instigation of unmerciful hunger, they would be urged to mutiny in the town, whereby the enemy might take hold ... and overwhelm us in a sudden and general destruction.

Despite all the 'threats and daily urgencies' that he received from the military command, the mayor 'still neglected to provide corn for those who had none, or mills to grind for those who yet had some left'.

By 2 August the anonymous chronicler of the siege wrote in his diary: 'The town was now in a miserable condition. The soldiers searched and rifled the houses of the inhabitants for victuals. They had lived on horse flesh for several weeks and most of that as lean as carrion'. There was also no salt to preserve the meat, which meant that epidemic sickness was rampant; 'Many died of fluxes [dysentery].' This was the picture within the garrison; among the civilian population, without the umbrella of army organisation and discipline, things declined at a far swifter rate. A week into August and the townspeople had become what he described as 'very uneasy towards the soldiers'. The Earl of Norwich, at the suggestion of Mayor Cooke, asked Fairfax to allow the civilians to leave 'that they might not perish', although he must have known what the reply would be. Although the inhabitants too begged to be allowed to 'fly to your Christian clemency', Fairfax predictably turned them down adding that he did 'pity the condition

30. Sir Thomas Fairfax refused to allow hundreds of starving civilians to leave Colchester, driving them back into the town, where they joined the clamour for its immediate surrender, grim evidence that his war of attrition was working at last.

of yourselves and your town'. For him it was a grimly satisfying omen of that his patient war of attrition was working.

The siege diarist watched the tension build among the desperate population:

> The poor of the town, having quite exhausted their provisions, began to throng together making great clamours and exclamations of their being ill used and falling into necessity.

There were daily confrontations outside garrison headquarters, including women with their children 'who lay howling and crying on the ground for bread'. By 12 August this situation was getting completely out of hand: 'The rabble got together a vast crowd ... clamouring for surrender and they did this every evening'. The troops 'beat off the men, but the women and children would not stir, bidding the soldiers kill them, saying they would rather be shot than starved'. Carter maintained that Sir Charles Lucas was much moved by the plight of 'his own town's born people' and urged the council of war to release precious stocks of corn from the garrison's 'general store house' and a ration was indeed issued to 'every family according to the number of people in it'. It was a necessary move to head off an even more serious riot, but one with far-reaching consequences for the future. Carter pointed out that 'half that quantity would have supported us [the garrison] till we had obtained better conditions from the enemy than we did'. Even so this release of precious food stocks to civilians could only be a stop-gap measure. Things were bound to get worse.

Desertions from the garrison began to increase, as soldiers slipped over the walls in the dead of night, risking the firing squad if they were caught. 'Several hundred got out', said the diarist, 'and either passed the enemy's guards or surrendered to them', claiming the clemency offered by Fairfax to the rank and file who quit. Six such deserters came in with accounts of deepening divisions between the townspeople and the military and even within the ranks of the garrison itself. They claimed that the 'chief officers' still dined well off three-quarters of a pound of beef *per diem*, while the rest went hungry. 'For the most part', said one, 'we eat nothing but rye bread and water, though [there is] much wine in the town with which the officers make merry'. They maintained that the population were 'infinitely weary of their company'. Lord Goring and Lord Capel 'carry things high and peremptory', although Sir Charles, the local man, was thought 'more moderate'. All the flour was being comandeered by the military 'which doth reduce the townsmen to extreme misery for want of bread'. The Parliament-leaning *Moderate Intelligencer* thought that the garrison was indeed fortunate to eat 'stinking' horse flesh: 'we cannot conceive what is eaten by the poorer sort ... it must be famine that must get us in the town'. The same paper carried the story of how one malcontented Parliamentary trooper had defected to Colchester pretending to be a messenger from Langdale's northern rebels, promising them imminent relief. Such was the euphoria he produced that he was wined and dined lavishly, before being exposed and thrown in gaol where 'all that he could say could not save him'.

Carter dismissed the image of drunken, overfed Cavaliers carousing while Colchester burned, as the predictable lies of treacherous turncoats, anxious to ingratiate themselves with the other side. He recalled

> horse flesh to be as precious to us as the choicest meats before; the soldiers, all the officers and gentlemen, from the lords to the lowest degree eating nothing else, unless cats and dogs.

Each soldier, he said, saved some of his bread ration to attract passing dogs which he then brained with the butt of his musket: 'I have known six shillings given for the side of a dog, and yet but a small one neither ... nor was there, in a short time, a dog left'. The town was ransacked 'for all things eatable' and often turned up unexpected hordes of spices, oils and starch which, when put together, 'made very good puddings'.

However some passable horseflesh was found and 'a bottle or two of wine' when Lady Katherine Scott was allowed to approach the defences on 10 August to give the Earl of Norwich the news, personally, that his wife had died. It was a 'collation ... which they ate heartily on and liked', as they stood at the ramparts in no-man's-land, with officers from both sides, though it is not recorded if they were told what sort of meat it was they were eating. Carter also insisted that the members of the Parliamentary county committee, who were still being held hostage, enjoyed the best of food, 'being allowed to receive any provisions of fresh and hot meats, as vension pasties, into the town, without the least opposition or affront'. To the garrison, however, horse flesh remained

> so delicious a food among the soldiers, that we could scarcely secure our horses in the stables, for every morning one stable or other was robbed and our horses knocked on the head and sold in the shambles by the pound.

All these details, and more, were followed avidly in taverns and markets places up and down the country, but especially in nearby London and the other big cities, by a public baying for infomation – any information at all – about the progress of the war. This crisis had turned Britain, almost overnight, into a nation of newspaper addicts. The demand to know what was going on created a thiving and violently partisan media industry. Everyone who could read, or could get someone to read to them, snapped up any printed material they could lay their hands on. The battle was on for the hearts and minds of a whole section of people who only lately had been dismissed as insignificant in the political process. Now for the first time, and all too briefly for them, the extremities of circumstance had made their opinions vital to the country's future.

THE PRESS

The Second Civil War, and the siege of Colchester in particular, saw a vigorous resurgence of the propaganda battle which had begun with the

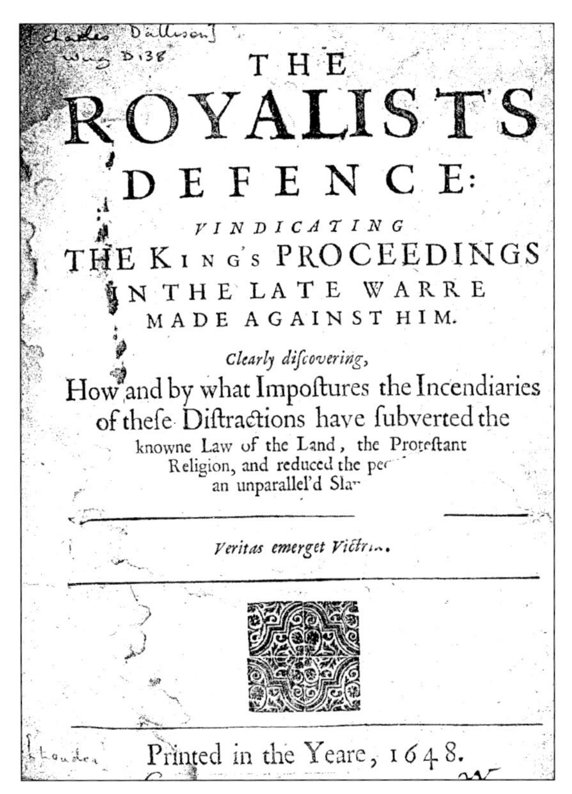

THE
ROYALISTS
DEFENCE:
VINDICATING
THE KING's PROCEEDINGS
IN THE LATE WARRE
MADE AGAINST HIM.

Clearly diſcovering,

How and by what Impoſtures the Incendiaries
of theſe Diſtractions have ſubverted the
knowne Law of the Land, the Proteſtant
Religion, and reduced the pe[...]
an unparallel'd Sla[...]

Veritas emerget Victr[...]

Printed in the Yeare, 1648.

31. Propaganda became a potent weapon used by both sides in the war. Here the Royalists laid out their justification for going to war for a second time, claiming that it was Parliament and not the King who had 'subverted the law of the land' and reduced the population to a state of 'slavery'. (Essex County Council)

breakdown of royal government in 1640. In the anarchy of the war years, when government censorship became virtually non-existent, at least 23,000 pamphlets, newsbooks, sermons, speeches and ballads were published, all carrying a potent political message. This surpassed even the output of the French Revolution a century later. By 1645 there were in circulation every week sixteen newsbooks, or as we would call them now, newspapers. Each was partisan in the extreme and sold anything between 500 and 3,000 copies. Demand for news was insatiable and feeding it quickly became a very profitable industry. For the first time the workings of politics were exposed to the gaze of the 'rude rabble', those outside the exclusive world of the ruling elite, much to the disgust of even progressive Presbyterian intellectuals like Richard Baxter. He feared for the future when it was left to the:

> ignorant, who cannot rule themselves; and the vicious that are enemies and hinderers of piety; and the worldlings that mind nothing but what is under their feet and have no time to think of heaven.

He despaired that 'these must be our sovereigns'.

Numb. 2.

The Colcheſter Spie.

Truly informing the Kingdome of the eſtate of that gallant Town, and the attempts of *Fairfax* againſt it: with ſome other remarkable Intelligence from the Engliſh and Scots Army; the laſt news from the Navie, alſo from Weſtminſter and London.

From *Thurſday, Aug.* 10. to *Thurſday, Aug.* 17. 1648.

Yet Colcheſter bears bravely up,
They eat and drink apace,
Lately they gave a deadly cup
Unto the Babes of Grace.

Though the Saints hope to ſtarve them out,
Alas it nere will bee:
For if they grapple t'other bout,
O *Fairfax*, farewell thee.

To the Earl of Norwich, Lord Capell, Sir Charles Lucas, and the reſt of the renowned Captaines in Colcheſter.

Shrink not brave Hero's, be not you diſmaid,
Becauſe ſo long you want your hoped aid;
You know it is not eaſie to bring downe,
Traytors who ſit at Helme, and graſp a Crowne:
The Scots muſt force their way, through Lamberts heart.
And ſend ten thouſand for to claime their part,
Amongſt the Furies, ere they can come on
with winged haſt, to your redemption;
The Prince of *Wales*, although King of the Seas,
Yet feares his cure may adde to their Diſeaſe;
Should he act raſhly, and a Battaile trie
Ere things are come unto maturitie,
Things work apace, be patient and ere long
Unto your reſcue comes three Armies ſtrong.

Printed in the Yeer 1648.

32. Allegations of war crimes proliferated as the siege worsened: many were reported – and often distorted – in the newspapers of the day. Repeated attempts to censor the press failed and 'news books' produced by both sides circulated widely. The *Colchester Spie* bolstered the Royalist cause with heroic couplets. (Essex County Council)

This print revolution was an insidious challenge to the established social order when:

> at ordinary and common tables, where they have scarce money to pay for their dinner, [they] enter politic discourses of princes, kingdoms and estates ... talking of wars of Christendom, the honour of their country and such like treasons.

Even though two-thirds of men and nine-tenths of women were unable even write their names, literacy was spreading relentlessly downwards through the social strata. It was helped by the Puritan revolution in religion, where the ability to read the scriptures was considered the individual's high road to heaven. With the Civil War factions so finely balanced between King and Parliament, the

The Parliaments *Scrich-Owle*, *Numb* 1.

Her ſinging before' death.

O R

Intelligence from ſeveral parts of the kingdom touching
Affaires, Humors, Projects, Conditions,
Aimes, and Deſigns &c.

Of the *Parliament* and *Army*.

Rebellion now's at a ſtand;
The *Houſes* they do feare,
Their latter dayes are nere at hand,
To welcome in the yeare.

For *Cromwell* he is dead and gon,
And buried at St. *Gyles*,
And *Fairfax* he is glad to run,
From *Goring*, full ten *Miles*.

Put up your Pipes and *Vote no more*,
Take up your packs be *ganging*,
Or th' *Devill* elſe will pay his ſcore,
And ſend you all to hanging.

Whether by *Sea*, or *Land it is*,
Your voyage you doe take,
The worſt I wiſh, you may not miſſe,
Deſtruction (for your ſake.)

Your monſtrous deeds I mean to tell,
In theſe few following *Lines*,
No Mortalls can them *Parllell*,
Your equals muſt be F I N D E S.

Quis vetat hoc verum? ——

Printed in the firſt year of the deceaſe of King *Oliver* 1648

33. The very first edition of another Royalist paper, the *Parliaments Scritch-Owle*, trumpeted the Royalist cause through verse. (Essex County Council)

ensuing propaganda battle for the uncommitted among the British public was ferocious. Scurrilous tracts, even before the war, threw convention and caution to the wind, deriding the King and his counsellors. Charles was variously called a knave, a bastard, a papist and a stuttering fool – even a murderer.

The new, highly competitive newspaper industry was soon staffed-up by craftsmen and tradesmen only too anxious to try their hand at a new enterprise. Most were hacks, plain and simple, attracted by the quick money to be made. Although many Royalists sneered at this new breed of journalist it was not long before the King himself was forced to follow the trend to improve his image among a wider public. Soon his newspapers were being snapped up on the enemy-occupied streets of London, despite all the efforts of the Parliamentary censors to stop them. John Milton likened the censor to the farmer who 'thought to pound up crows by shutting his park gate'.

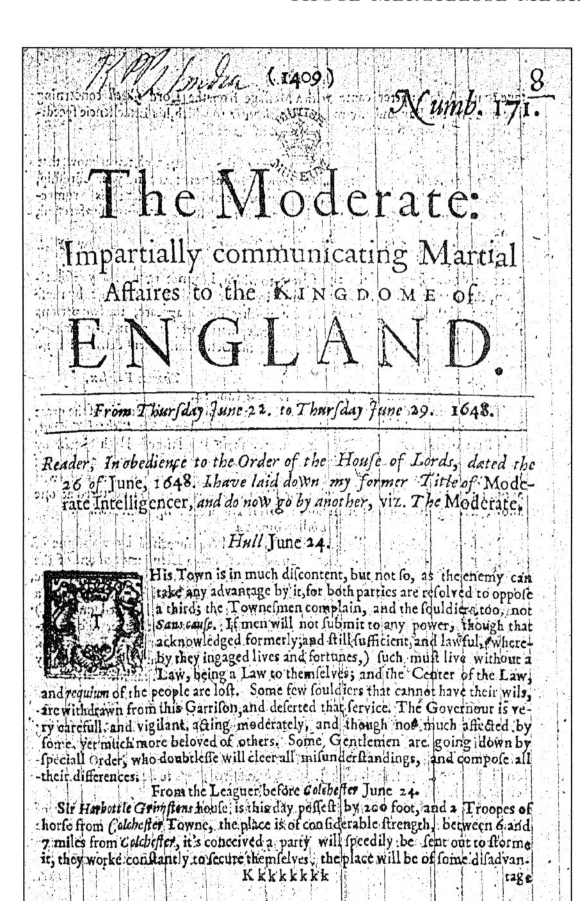

(1409) 8

Numb. 171.

The Moderate:

Impartially communicating Martial Affaires to the KINGDOME of ENGLAND.

From Thursday June 22. to Thursday June 29. 1648.

Reader; In obedience to the Order of the House of Lords, dated the 26 *of* June, 1648. *I have laid down my former Title of* Moderate Intelligencer, *and do now go by another,* viz. *The* Moderate.

Hull June 24.

This Town is in much discontent, but not so, as the enemy can take any advantage by it, for both parties are resolved to oppose a third; the Townesmen complain, and the souldiers too, not *Sans cause*. If men will not submit to any power, though that acknowledged formerly, and still sufficient, and lawful, (whereby they ingaged lives and fortunes,) such must live without a Law, being a Law to themselves; and the Center of the Law, and *requium* of the people are lost. Some few souldiers that cannot have their wils, are withdrawn from this Garrison, and deserted that service. The Governour is very carefull and vigilant, acting moderately, and though not much affected by some, yet much more beloved of others. Some Gentlemen are going down by speciall Order, who doubtlesse will cleer all misunderstandings, and compose all their differences.

From the Leaguer before *Colchester* June 24.

Sir *Harbottle Grimstons* house, is this day possest by 200 foot, and 2 Troopes of horse from *Colchester* Towne, the place is of considerable strength, between 6 and 7 miles from *Colchester*, it's conceived a party will speedily be sent out to storme it, they worke constantly to secure themselves, the place will be of some disadvantage

Kkkkkkkk

34. The *Moderate* took a more responsible approach to the news, supporting Parliament. It was often sympathetic as well to the Levellers. (Essex County Council)

Inflammatory tracts mercilessly mocked official attempts to track down their publishers. New titles proliferated. *Mercurius Psitacus, the Parrotting Mercury*, in only its fourth edition, taunted the government censors: 'O how grates their patience that they cannot lay claws upon me'; and referring to the practice of smuggling hot news in the folds of ladies' skirts added, 'let me alone I say, and suffer me peaceably to lie hidden in the plackets of my she-Hawkers without ferreting'.

Claims and counter-claims were traded weekly and black propaganda was a weapon in constant use. Stories were constantly leaked to the media, some founded on fact, many merely unchecked fiction. It was amazing how fast news travelled and now, with Parliament in disarray, the Royalists almost at the gates of London and the King poised once more to turn military defeat into political victory, the war of words reached a new frenzy. Each side was obsessed with the intensifying the inhumanity of the struggle and the brutality and cruelty of their opponents. The siege of Colchester produced repeated claims of torture, rape, extortion and arson, as well as kidnapping, reprisal killings, and mass murder. All were accompanied by charges of treachery and pillage on a grand scale, both official and unofficial.

WAR CRIMES

The terms 'rebel' and 'traitor' in the Second Civil War were interchangeable, depending on one's allegiance; so too was the definition of what constituted a war crime and a crime against the people, whose rights both sides were claiming to defend. For the soldiers of the New Model Army, and the 'Saints' of the godly nation, the worst offender was the King himself, 'that man of blood', whose continued arrogance in the face of divine judgement had caused the renewed fighting in the first place. At Colchester the traitors who backed him were condemned for ruthlessly holding an entire civilian community to ransom. The pamphlet *Colchester Teares*, brought out in London at the end of July, bitterly condemned the Royalists for taking shelter behind a innocent human shield:

> what was the cause of your flying into a walled town when (if your cause, courage, and consciences had been right) you might have fought it out with the choice and advantage of your own ground, and ... have trusted God ... Why do you use that poor town so hardly and your enemies so gently ... before ever you had tried your own strength?

The newspaper claims became particularly partisan and vitriolic over the alleged abuses of human rights by their opponents. *Colchester Teares* claimed 'credible reports' of 'outrages committed in town'. There were tales of rape: 'much filthiness might be named of women ... sending their husbands out forcibly and fall[ing] on their wives in their absence.' All ranks of the garrison were tainted. Even Sir Charles Lucas himself 'had ensnared a woman, if my Lord Goring [the Earl of Norwich] had not come in', and a maid, defending her mistress against assault by troops, had had lighted matches applied to her fingertips. Pregnant women and children, too, had been 'turned out of doors and into the crossfire'. The Royalist *Colchester Spie*, which made only a brief appearance on the streets of London, in turn charged the Parliamentary forces with torture, even the tender age of the victims made no difference to the inhumanity of their treatment. It claimed on 11 August that a fourteen-year-old boy, suspected of taking a message from Lord Goring to the Scots, was burned with matches, half-hanged several times and then suspended over a fire until he was 'black all over like an Ethiope, crying out with horrible yells'. The *Moderate*, aware of the brutal realities of war and sympathetic as always to the army, insisted that the boy had merely been threatened with hanging and that he received punishment only after he had turned down the painless option of a bribe for the information he had. They did admit that they 'burnt his fingers with match' and also conceded that all this apparently took place in the presence of Lord General Fairfax himself.

The Roundheads, lying in the trenches of the leaguer, were accused of using starving civilians for target practice when they ventured over the walls of Colchester in search of food. The *Parliament Kite* reported:

> Many poor people would go out of the town to glean corn at harvest time, but such is the cruelty of the Saints, that they not only denies them, but make nothing to shoot poor old women, and other feeble persons that venture out for relief of themselves and their families.

The paper claimed one piece of macabre justice when: 'A soldier shot a woman the other day that happened to be his own mother'.

Atrocity allegations against the Royalists also included charges that the defenders were being ordered to fire poisoned bullets and what today would be termed dum-dum bullets – slugs with their edges deliberately toughened to maximise their damage to human flesh. They were said to be chewed by the marksmen before firing them. The charges, categorically denied by Norwich and the Royalist leaders, caused waves of anger among Parliamentarian troops and led to vengeance being visited on Royalist prisoners. The *Moderate Intelligencer* reported that some Royalist troops had been captured in possession of '6 or 7 poisoned bullets'; many having been 'cast with sand being a thing contrary to the law of arms'. Fairfax had warned that retaliatory action 'will follow' if these crimes continued. His troops too were said to be 'exasperated with the loss of blood of their fellows', and they reacted violently when one of their popular senior officers, Colonel Shambrook was 'shot in the body, the bullet since taken out, and we find it poisoned, boiled in coprice'. When, the following day, Colonel Shambrook died of his wounds, reprisals were reported: 'Many of

A

LETTER

SENT

To the Honorable *William Lenthal* Eſq;
Speaker of the Honorable Houſe of Commons,

Of the late

Fight at Colcheſter,

AND,

How the Suburbs of the ſaid Town
were fired by

The Lord *Goring*, Lord *Capel*, Sir
Charls Lucas, and the reſt of the Enemy.

PRinted by the Command of the Honorable
William Lenthal *Eſq; Speaker of the Honorable Houſe of Commons.*

London, Printed for *Edward Huſband*, Printer to the
Honorable Houſe of Commons, *July* 17. 1648.

35. Fire – a constant nightmare in the mainly wooden-built towns of the time – caused widespread damage to the extensive suburbs of Colchester. Often the fires were started deliberately, for strategic reasons, to deny the opposition cover from which to attack. The extent of the damage shocked the rest of the country. Here a Parliamentary pamphlet blames the garrison for starting the blaze. (Essex County Council)

the prisoners we took yesterday are likewise dead of those wounds and cuts they received, merely for their using poisoned bullets, who otherwise had received fair quarter'. The *Moderate Intelligencer* reckoned that twenty of them were 'slain upon the place, most of them gents as is conceived by their good apparel and white skins'. Carter did admit that the rough and ready conditions under which the bullets were manufactured posed a problem, but there had been no deliberate intention by the garrison to break the rules of warfare. The *Parliament Kite* also dismissed the charges: 'The town bullets be as bad as poison to them which makes the Roundheads cry out poison bullets, poison bullets'.

The 'crime' which especially horrified everyone was the extent of the damage inflicted on the once elegant town of Colchester by fire. The country was aghast, despite becoming well used to such scenes of wanton destruction in cities and farms across the land during the previous four years of war. Both sides were quick to accuse the other of barbarously torching

36. This section of St John's, lying next to the old town wall, was set alight in the fighting, and in some of these houses, rebuilt shortly after the siege, evidence has been found of that original conflagration.

large sections of its once fine suburbs, reducing them to ashes. The truth was that the pair of them were to blame, both bowing to the relentless pressure of what they considered military necessity. Colchester, thus far isolated from the direct havoc of the Civil War, was hopelessly unprepared for its literal baptism of fire.

The prospect of fire in the closely packed wooden buildings of an early modern town was an abiding horror in the seventeenth century. Less than twenty years later Europe watched in morbid awe as the ultimate atrocity of the Great Fire consumed London. In the days before insurance, fire could reduce both rich and poor to total ruin overnight. The arsonist was an arch-terrorist who could bring instant panic to the streets. In France fire-raisers were burned at the stake along with witches and heretics; if fire broke out the already recognised bogey-men of society were instantly suspected of starting it, whatever the real cause. Papist agents were often favourites in times of national emergency; in Colchester six years before, on the eve of the Civil War, special night watches for incendiaries were on the look out for Irishmen allegedly, Charles Stuart's new and sinister allies. Rumours of their phantom presence touched off riots in 1642. Nightmare became reality on the night of 15 July when the flames raged all night on the south side of town. According to one eye witness: 'Some of us a being a mile distant had light almost to read a letter; a terrible red dusky, bloody cloud seemed to hang over the town ... accompanied by lamentable outcries of men women and children'. The *Perfect Weekly Account* on 19 July reported that it was 'the saddest spectacle that hath been seen of that kind since the wars began'. The *Moderate's* correspondent agreed that it was 'so fearful and horrid a sight, as seldom the like ever seen in England before'.

Premeditated criminal intent was naturally attributed to the other side. The *Perfect Weekly Account* blamed the Royalist defenders who it alleged had set the fires to cover their retreat:

> The enemy is so enraged at his loss (having totally by this means shut themselves up within the walls) that they set the suburbs around the town on fire ... by this we conceive that they are desperately bent, and will even burn also the town before they yield. I hope in the Lord he will enable us very shortly to gain the place, and make such destroyers of the Nation examples to posterity.

Mercurius Britannicus described the Royalists as 'Nero like' delighting in the flames. The more sober *Moderate Intelligencer* did point out: 'The enemy [Royalists] burnt some houses in the Heath to keep our men from taking advantage of them'. The Royalist *Mercurius Psitacus*, of course, made a virtue out of it: 'the valiant Colchesterians have been compelled to burn down the suburbs of the town, so that when they [the army] next approach they must look for a more hot and desperate service than ever'.

But still *Mercurius Melancholicus* preferred to dish some black propaganda: 'It was Fairfax not the King's party who fired the suburbs of Colchester to endanger, and if twere possible to fire the city, for they took the time to fire when the wind was in the East'. The reason: 'Colchester hath been an eminent example of loyalty unto this whole kingdom'. *Colchester Teares* accused the garrison of turning a 'needless' tactical device into a protection racket by demanding between £14 and £50 from householders in return for not torching their properties, 'and then presently have fired the same houses themselves and lay the fault upon the Roundheads'. The result, it said, was that 'they turned them and theirs (without so much as letting them time to take out their goods and wares) a begging to the wide world'. It was a charge that Carter was at pains to deny: to mitigate the long-term damage he claimed they had even employed 'carpenters and other workmen' to pull down some houses near the town walls so that the 'materials might be preserved, and less prejudice done to the town and the owners'. The residents who still remained were also given the chance to 'convey away their goods first'. It was, if we can believe it, an exceptional example of forbearance in the heat of battle especially considering, as Carter himself says, 'we could not have maintained the town half an hour' had the houses remained standing. The Royalist *Mercurius Psitacus* insisted that the garrison commanders, Norwich, Capel, and Lucas, all men of substantial property, had 'pawned their estates to the townsmen, that they should not be the least endamaged by this their necessitated fire, and that when his Majesty shall regain his own they will afford them ample satisfaction'. What, the paper demanded, 'can be more honourable?'

The morality, or otherwise, of taking hostages also provoked a storm of self-righteous controversy, mainly because both sides were guilty of breaching what were considered the acceptable standards of civilised behaviour. It will be recalled that almost all of Parliament's Essex committee, with Sir William Masham at their head, had been hijacked at Chelmsford before the siege started, and taken along by the rebel army to Colchester. The move was seen by pro-Parliamentary pamphleteers as a 'desperate' one: 'the enemy thinks to get conditions for themselves, by their having Sir William Masham and others of the Committee prisoners'. Although some of the Royalist press maintained they were being kept 'in reasonable conditions' others were perfectly happy to gloat over the callous treatment that they admitted Masham had sometimes received in custody. *Mercurius Bellicus* described with brutal relish how the Earl of Norwich 'keeps him (Masham) fasting and dark and now and then brings him out, to make sport,... (presuming on his hunger) tying a crust to a string, make him leap and snap at it'. Although there was constant talk of trading Sir William for a leading Royalist prisoner, nothing came of it. But the hostage stakes were raised by Parliament when they ordered the retaliatory arrest of several prominent Royalists, including the Laudian Bishop of Ely Matthew Wren. However, more controversially, the teenage son and heir of Colchester's aristocratic defender, Lord Capel was also arrested at the family home. Taking this young man provoked a howl of protest.

The Royalist version ran thus: the honourable Lord Capel, threatened with prison.for 'not compounding so long as the King is without his crown, leaving his pious and dear Lady great with child', went to Colchester to rejoin the colours. He:

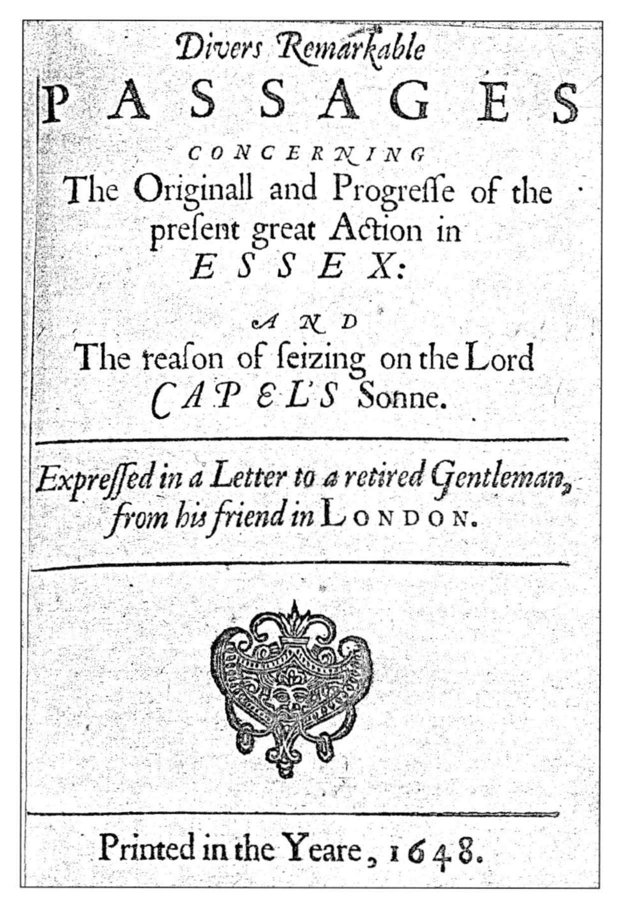

Divers Remarkable
PASSAGES
CONCERNING
The Originall and Progresse of the
present great Action in
ESSEX:
AND
The reason of seizing on the Lord
CAPEL'S Sonne.

Expressed in a Letter to a retired Gentleman,
from his friend in LONDON.

Printed in the Yeare, 1648.

37. Accusations of kidnapping, abduction, torture and extortion were common. The Royalists were criticised for taking hostage members of the government's county committee and holding them, like human shields, in Colchester. Here a pamphlet justifies the arrest and detention of Lord Capel's teenage son by way of reprisal. The boy was later released after vigorous protests to Parliament by his mother. (Essex County Council)

> could not conceive it possible, that any who wore the shapes of men or called gentlemen would offer, or suffer to be afforded anything unworthy to such a Lady, and in her condition, or to any of his innocent and harmless children.

He was wrong. According to the *Colchester Spie*, the arrested youth was taken to Colchester as a bargaining chip for Sir William Masham's release or, worse still, to use him as a human shield 'before the mouth of the enemy's cannon'. Masham, on the other hand, was painted as a 'mischievous person, old in wickedness, and though no prisoner of war, yet a prime author of it,... arrested for his faults, by those whose servant he was'. Capel's sixteen-year-old heir, by contrast, was a 'young Gentleman, of a pure and candid spirit, of a sweet and gracious disposition, who knows no evil, nor ever did, or intended hurt to the County of Essex, or any creature'. Lord Capel's reply to suggestions that he exchange Masham for his son was unequivocal:

he 'disdained the motion'. Eventually it was reported by *Mercurius Psitacus* that Lady Capel got the boy's release by petitioning Parliament, where she succeeded in convincing 'their Monsterships' that such retaliation against her husband was 'contrary to the rules of honour'.

Lady Capel's courage in defence of the family honour, and civilised behaviour in general, was praised by the Royalist press who contrasted it coarsely with the allegedly gross conduct of another of the Essex committee prisoners, Mr Sampson Sheffield. His craven behaviour on arrest was detailed by *Mercurius Elencticus*:

> when [he was] taken prisoner amongst the rest at Chelmsford, did that very day beshit himself, no less than three several times: they thought that he had shit in policy more than necessity, of purpose to be quit of them, but they found that it was Parliamentary fear that possessed him: so they got the nasty varlet made clean but what a pickle he may be now in, judge all men.

The Perfect Weekly Account, in the meantime, was also claiming human-shield status for Sir William Masham:

> The enemy [Royalists] fearing that his Excellency [Fairfax] would suddenly fall to storm the town, they brought out Sir W. Masham and others of the Committee and let them on the walls at such places where they expected the cannon to play.

This brought Royalist denials as they painted a black picture indeed of the Parliamentary *parvenu.* He was apparently forever calling for 'wine and plenty of dainties in this besieged place which he wont to abound in Westminster' and it was said that he suggested, in a message to Fairfax, that 'some of the wives, children and friends of those who had him in bondage, might be seized on as prisoners'. The General was apparently 'more of a soldier' than to agree, but Parliament took up the suggestion anyway. The escalation of hostage-taking led to further financial pressure being applied to the so-called 'delinquent' Royalists, pressure that many considered was illegal. Once again Parliament was laying itself open to charges of arbitrary and dictatorial government, far worse than anything Charles Stuart imposed on the country.

THE BURDENS OF WAR

Old-established monarchists complained bitterly that they were being placed in double jeopardy by a cash-strapped, and totally unrepresentative, government which was only managing to cling to power courtesy of the army. *Mercurius Bellicus* complained on 27 June that unrepentant Royalists, who had already been fined by the victors for their past convictions, 'shall have new fines set upon their heads, and this they call excellent justice'. While the burden of war was crippling Parliament, the siege of Colchester was turning into a catastrophe, not only for the town, but for the entire county of Essex because of the collateral damage that it was causing. The Royalist *Parliamentary Kite* spoke for many when it said:

> The Country of Essex is much annoyed with the two-legg'd caterpillars that devours their young fruits ... They [Parliamentary troops] look like Pharaoh's lean kine, as if they had eat one another and shit themselves out again ... The country deny to send them in provisions, and though the Saints can preach by the spirit they cannot live by the Spirit.

The local population, facing the mounting challenge of going about their daily lives, were heartily sick of both sides. Parliamentary pamphlets like, *A Fight* complained of the 'plundering and outrageous deportments of the Cavaliers', who, on arrival, had promised to protect the local population from 'harm and damage [and] yet they are plundered by them as much as any others. The civil women and maids are afraid to go out of their houses'.

Fairfax had made good discipline an early priority for the New Model Army, placing great importance on paying the troops and eliminating a major cause of pillage. They were expected to pay for what they required from the local population. In the first war this policy had been repaid handsomely in civilian cooperation. In fact, the rank and file themselves were keenly aware of the extra suffering that their free quarter could impose on an already hard-pressed population and had long suspected that their pay was being deliberately withheld by Parliament as part of an orchestrated campaign to undermine their popularity prior to disbanding them completely. Army propagandists were at pains to emphasise the strict disciplinary code which controlled their troops. The 'straggling soldiers of his [Fairfax's] army' were warned on arrival at Colchester against 'plunder and abuse of the country and outrages'. The orders of the day demanded a roll-call of troops twice every twenty-four hours and that 'henceforth no soldier or officer do presume to straggle a mile from the leaguer, or stir away from their colours and duty, under pain of severely being proceeded against under the Articles of War'.

But however strict the discipline the demands of war were voracious and deeply unpopular. In mid-July one Royalist pamphlet highlighted the scale of the problem. The army was 'forcing the Country against their wills to join with them; and fetching their provision daily from them without paying anything for the same'. Often the army claimed financial contributions in lieu of produce: 'one town (within twelve miles of them) is at £36 a week for food for them; and so are all others proportionally charged'. Recruiting demands on local manpower were also considered exorbitant: 'the unwilling country are made to help forward their own destruction, and driven on (they say) as Turkish slaves are, to be food for the bullet'. Damage was also great to extensive stands of corn being trampled down and all this taking place 'in that county which hath been so constantly faithful to the Parliament from the very beginning ... Now it is apparent what the reward and wages is'. The warning was plain for all to read: ''tis conceived that every other county shall be made to drink of that cup'.

In this overheated atmosphere there were many tales of individual outrages, often involving class rivalries. Local officials were often accused of abusing their new found positions of trust. A typical incident was reported by Royalist *Mercurius Elencticus*: 'They took occasion to rob village and country, as they did with Master Mumford at Hatfeld Brodock [Hatfield Broad Oak], near Sawbridgeworth in Essex'. Here it was said they

> took horses, plate and money and when they had done, broke his daughter's finger to get off her ring. This was the religious acts of him they call Colonel Ewres, a quondam neighbour of Mr Mumford's, one that in times of peace was a poor beggarly villain, whose credit never extended beyond a jug of beer.

The message from hostile pamphleteers and newsbook editors was that Fairfax was desperately hanging on and receiving precious little help from Westminster to do it:

> his Excellency send post upon post, message upon message, intimating that if he be not speedily recruited both with men and money the holy war must needs end ... they have opened their heavy case to their cash-keepers of the City'.

38. Edmund Ludlow, a leading Republican: he made a special trip to Colchester to warn Fairfax about the plots of some MPs in Parliament to betray the sacrifices of the army in the field and go behind its back to make a separate peace with the King. He failed to persuade the General to lead a *coup d'état* against them.

A letter, it was reported, had even gone to Parliament from Fairfax's secretary John Rushworth sarcastically highlighting the problem: 'If the news of any success this army hath were acceptable, you would send one weeks pay to an Army that hath not had one penny this month. J.R.'. The implications for Colchester and its inhabitants, should they surrender to such an unpaid rabble, was obvious: 'his gouty-hocked Excellency hath promised them [his soldiers] that it will rain gold and silver this day sevennight, that they shall equally divide the plunder of Colchester, and make themselves rich by other men's losses'. The propaganda message was clear: pillage and plunder would soon be the only method of sustaining the Parliamentary war effort, and it was one that worried the increasingly radical troops of the New Model Army. Many of them needed no convincing that they were already being stabbed in the back by a growing number of defeatist MPs at Westminster – men who had begun negotiating a fresh deal with the King.

THE NATION'S RUIN

Throughout the siege at Colchester, and elsewhere on the war's many fronts, the troops of Parliament suffered from the uncomfortable feeling that they were being betrayed by their own politicians, many more of whom were coming around to the idea of restoring the monarch, unfettered by any conditions, and getting rid of them preferably without pay. Fairfax had been warned about the peace party's manoeuvres in mid-August by friends in the House of Lords, who were demanding from him 'some speedy course in reducing Colchester' otherwise they would not be able to head-off moves to sign an early truce with the King. Those in favour of a quick treaty were also spreading scare stories about the growing hostility of the army towards Parliamentary moderates and the civil population in general. There were terrifying predictions of an imminent military coup and the imposition of martial law which were, in this uncertain climate, all too frighteningly credible. A pamphlet in July entitled, *A Discovery of the Intentions of the Army*, confidently predicted – and with uncanny accuracy as it turned out – that:

> when the army hath beaten Colchester, and all the rising Counties, they will go to the House of Commons, and pull out one hundred of them, and put in others of their own choosing, and then they will divide and share the Kingdom between them.

Then, as now, journalists could sometimes be justly proud of their prophesies – and their scoops. On 15 August *Mercurius Pragmaticus* claimed that a:

> Messenger was sent to the leaguer before Colchester, informing his Excellency [Fairfax] that now was the time (or never) to draw off, and march towards London, to fetch down the privileges of the city and those creatures of the prerogative into an obedience of the Army.

The story was confirmed later by Edmund Ludlow in his memoirs.

Ludlow explained that 'by the advice of some friends I went down to the army, which lay at the time before Colchester to acquaint him [Fairfax] with the state of affairs at London'. Here he said 'a design was driving on to betray the cause in which so many people's blood had been shed'. The King, he warned, would never consider that he was bound by any treaty he made while still being kept 'under restraint' and would not 'account himself obliged by any thing he should promise under such circumstances'. Those in Parliament 'who pushed on the treaty with the greatest vehemency', said Ludlow, 'intended not that he [the King] should be bound to the performance of it'. The whole design he was sure, was to 'destroy the army; who, as they had assumed the power, ought to make best use of it, and to prevent the ruin of themselves and the nation'. Ludlow got a non-committal reaction from Fairfax to his call for direct military intervention in the political arena; he considered him to be 'irresolute', but while he was at Colchester the Republican got the agreement of the Commissary General, Henry Ireton, also serving in the leaguer, that 'it was necessary for the army to interpose in this matter'. Even at this stage, in mid-August, there was no question in radical minds about whether or not the army should intervene in the running of government – all they differed over was exactly when and how.

Vital in all these calculations was the formidable power wielded by the capital city and which way its leaders would jump in this crisis. After the First Civil War, the army on the one hand and the city of London on the other had superseded Parliament and the monarchy as the only remaining, truly functional institutions of the realm. In the on-going struggle for the political control of London the Presbyterians had emerged dominant. They had rid themselves of the old ruling elite and had no wish to restore the prewar political structure, but neither did they want to push the revolution any further. A quick and advantageous settlement with the King would consolidate their position, restore prosperity and hopefully get the army off their backs. The city was painfully aware of its vulnerability to military pressure. It had been occupied once already and remained convinced that the military was intent 'to possess themselves of, and be masters of the city of London'. Several Parliamentary pamphlets went out of their way to refute the stories. 'I can assure you', said one, 'they [the Army] have no such resolution, but are resolved to expedite northward, or to any other place where necessity shall require ... they have no thoughts of injury or prejudice against the city of London.' But Royalist rumours that marauding Parliamentary troops were about to fall on the city had an uncomfortable ring to them and many agreed that 'London hath good reason to pray for the safety of Colchester, for their Army resolve to look upon her next'.

Dealings with the capital had to be handled with kid gloves. *Mercurius Psitacus* noted that the fields around Colchester were littered with Parliamentary wounded, which 'Black Tom [Fairfax]' felt he could not send to London 'for fear of discouraging the citizens, who (as he hopes) will send out some regiments to join him'. Fairfax was no doubt also concerned with keeping the minds of the bankers clear of any images of defeat. He too must have been well aware of the stories of a powerful Royalist underground among the City's establishment. A letter, purportedly from Sir Marmaduke Langdale, the commander of the King's forces in possession of Carlisle, had been intercepted on its way to supporters in London. It urged them 'to be as active now as possible you can,... especially with those who are most eminent, and least to be suspected'. But Langdale warned: 'take heed how you discover too much to them until you get his Majesty to London and then you know what to do'.

But the Royalist hopes of high summer had taken several hard knocks. True a Scots army was now encamped on English soil and poised to march south, but many of the bush-fire rebellions against Parliament, which the Scots were due to stoke with their support, had already been put out. Only Colchester remained a substantial worry for the army. The latest newspaper to appear on the streets, the *Mercurius Anglicus*, chose to kick off its first edition on 3 August with the upbeat story that: 'They have good stores of sack and strong beer in the town to drink his majesty's health, when they shall be relieved by the Scots'. The grim reality was rather different.

5

THEY WILL NEVER FORGIVE YE

By mid-July the siege was over a month old, its misery increasing by the day. The Parliamentary press reported: 'We have cut off all their pipes for water ... [and] have furnished ourselves with a good store of lead' for bullets. 'They have very little water in the town, but what is muddy, or annoyed [polluted] with dead horses.' The captive Royalist cavalry, their main strike force, withered before their eyes. All available fodder was rapidly being used up and the animals were dying at an alarming rate. At least one-third of them had already been butchered for their meat. If the cavalry was to survive to fight another day, it would have to break-out, 'forcing a pass to advance into Suffolk by Nayland Bridge'. A council of war 'ordered that all the horse, excepting 200, should in the night sally forth and break through the leaguer to march northward in the hope of relief'. The garrison, with only fitful and inaccurate information reaching them about developments in the outside world, were pinning their hopes on Langdale's army in the north: 'at that time we had received great assurance, by private letters, that relief was intended and hasting towards us', said Carter.

Orders went out for a rendezvous of mounted men in the town's cattle-yard 'late in the night'. They were to be accompanied by 'a party of foot for

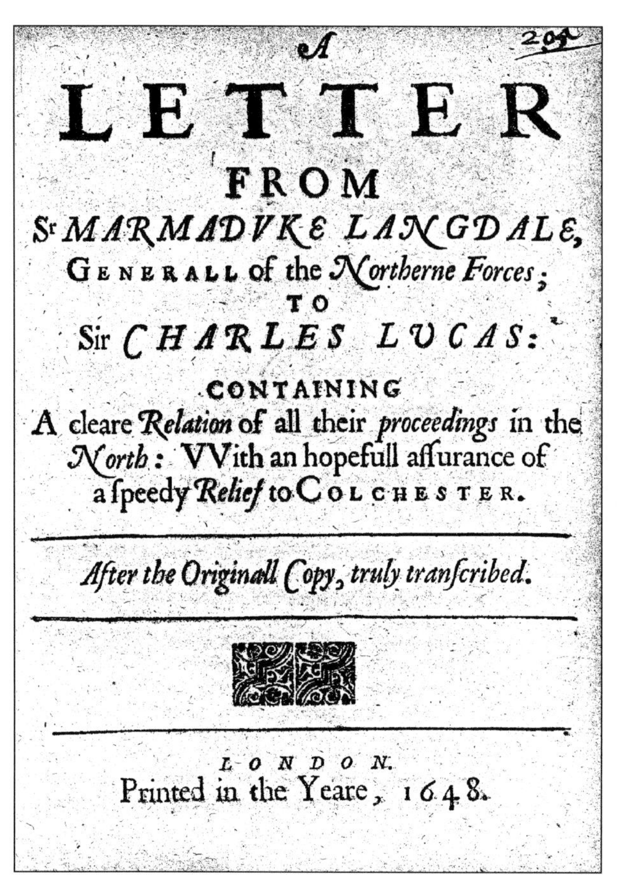
A
LETTER
FROM
Sr MARMADUKE LANGDALE,
GENERALL of the Northerne Forces;
TO
Sir CHARLES LUCAS:
CONTAINING
A cleare Relation of all their proceedings in the North: VVith an hopefull assurance of a speedy Relief to COLCHESTER.

After the Originall Copy, truly transcribed.

LONDON.
Printed in the Yeare, 1648.

39. The Colchester garrison lived in daily hope of relief from any one of a number of Royalist rebellions which broke out, in uncoordinated fashion, up and down the country. Much hope lay with Sir Marmaduke Langdale, the leader of a rising in the north. As this pamphlet revealed, Langdale was confident of linking up with an invading Scots army before marching to the 'speedy relief' of Colchester. Hopes were dashed when this 'Army of Engagement' was finally wiped out by Oliver Cromwell at Preston. (Essex County Council)

their assistance in forcing the enemy line'. The expedition got off to a promising start; they crossed the river by the Middle Mill and 'came within reach of the enemy sentinels before they were discovered, or any part of their [the army's] guards alarmed'. Then came disaster. The guides, 'who were for the most part townsmen', took the first opportunity to desert. They 'ran away immediately, the night being dark' leaving their charges lost, to fend for themselves. 'By [this] cowardly behaviour', said Carter, 'we were forced again into the town, which was done without the loss of a man, but it gave the enemy so much notice ... [that] it was afterwards not thought proper to make a second attempt'.

Even though the essential element of surprise was lost, some smaller detachments did succeed in getting out during the next week. According to the Colchester diarist, on 22 July:

> Two troops of royal horse sallied out at night resolved to break through or die. Without being perfectly discovered they went clean off and passing towards Tiptree Heath, and having good guides, they made their escape towards Cambridgeshire. [They] found means to disperse without being attacked, and went every man his own way as fate directed.

The army, he said, then reinforced their fortifications at the Middle Mill to 'prevent any more escapes that way'.

Once again Fairfax had stymied any aggressive initiative from within the beleaguered town, and his grip on the place was locked even harder by virtue of the fact that he was able to keep his numbers 'continually supplied [while] the besieged diminished'. The diarist recorded that the General sent in repeated offers of amnesty for the private soldiers prepared to surrender. Replying Norwich, Capel and Lucas sent him a letter in which they complained that it was not 'honourable or agreeable to the usage of war to offer conditions separately to the soldiers, exclusive of their officers and civilly desired his Lordship to send no more such messages or proposals or, if he did, he would not take it ill if they hanged the messenger'.

The little news that did filter into Colchester produced waves of brief optimism followed, almost immediately, by stories of subsequent disaster. At about this time a messenger managed to get through with word that 'there were so many strong parties up in arms for the King, and in so many places, that they would be very soon relieved'. The Colchester diarist wrote: 'This was caused to be read to the soldiers to encourage them'. Particularly heartening was the news of the Earl of Holland's rising at Kingston-upon-Thames and the fact that he, together with 500 horse, was heading their way. But within days 'we had notice that they were defeated and the Earl of Holland taken'. The effect on morale must have been devastating.

HEY FOR THE PRINCE OF WALES

The Colchester garrison, clutching at any straws of better news, now looked to the sea for relief, to the ships which had mutinied against Parliament and were now under the command of the eighteen-year-old Prince of Wales. It will be recalled (chapter 2) that the Royalist revolt in the navy had begun among eleven ships of the fleet lying at the Downs, off the east coast of Kent – the natural anchorage dominating the Thames Estuary. The castles at

A
FIGHT at SEA
Between the
Parliament Ships & thoſe that revolted,
AND
The boarding of ſome of the Parlia-
ment Ships, by a party from the three
Caſtles in KENT *that are kept for the King.*
And the ſtorming of *WAYMOR* Caſtle.
Alſo a bloody fight in *Ireland*. And a treaty of the Com-
manders of the Revolted ſhips with the Duke of YORKE.

LONDON
Printed for *H. Becke*, and are to be ſold in the
Old Bayley. 1648.

40. The Royalist revolt and the Second Civil War split the navy. Many ships mutinied and declared for the King. The Prince of Wales assumed command and threatened to use them to relieve Colchester and stage a foreign-backed landing on the south-east coast. However, his quarrelsome high command were incompetent and squandered their opportunities. (Essex County Council)

Walmer, Deal and Sandwich, overlooking and guarding the moorings, were taken in the King's name in May. The sailors were a notoriously conservative bunch of men; Clarendon described them as 'a nation by themselves rude and resolute in whatsoever they resolve'. They refused to take orders from their new vice-admiral, the Leveller Colonel Thomas Rainsborough – a soldier in the first war, though one with strong maritime connections and experience. The fiercely independent mariners suspected a conspiracy to turn them into a New Model Navy, with 'land soldiers in every ship, to master and overawe the seamen'. Many agreed with their old and popular admiral, William Batten – ousted from his post by Rainsborough – that 'a man should hold no command who openly professed himself to be a Leveller'. When Rainsborough, on 27 May, was rowed back to his ships, after inspecting the land installations, he was barred from re-boarding his own flagship and was lucky not to have been taken prisoner on the spot. A boatswain's mate was declared admiral in his stead. When the Kent rebellion collapsed at Maidstone, much of the vital shore-based support for the mutineers disappeared and the rebel ships were forced to sail for the port facilities of Holland, leaving behind the remainder still loyal to Parliament. The allegiance of the rest of the navy, based at Portsmouth, was also suspect. It left the Earl of Warwick, the Lord High Admiral, with no other choice but to confine them all to port. When, therefore, the Prince of Wales finally took his armada to sea again from Holland, at the beginning of July, it posed a potent and unopposed extra threat to Parliament. The rebel navy was a new and wild card in the game – no-one had any idea where or when it would strike.

The Prince of Wales made his first target the Downs. He aimed to relieve Deal and Walmer Castles, still holding-out against the New Model Army, and establish a bridgehead in England for a foreign invasion in support of the King. He tried an amphibious landing with some 1,500 men, but was forced 'back aboard' in the face of stiff opposition and sailed away. Now journalists began to speculate that he 'will strike again at some other place' and so early warnings sounded all over East Anglia, particularly to Harwich, Norwich and Yarmouth. Colchester saw in the fleet the tantalising prospect of imminent relief. One newspaper had it on good authority, on 19 July, that Sir Charles Lucas 'tells his soldiers that he hath received a message and declares that his Highness [the Prince of Wales] will send relief to them before Friday night'. A message, allegedly intercepted by the army on its way to Colchester from the rebel fleet, told the beleaguered garrison: 'if you hold out you are brave fellows. We drink your treble healths every day.'

Such news lifted the spirits of those trapped in Colchester. A Parliamentary pamphlet, on 17 July, said that 'The enemy in the town begins to grow far more insolent ... expecting supplies from Holland', despite the blockade which had been established in the mouth of the Colne River. The sad reality, however, reflected once more the hesitant, half-hearted and unco-ordinated leadership which was the serial curse of the Royalist cause both at sea and on dry land. Captured correspondence from Sir Anthony St Leger, who was serving with the Prince's fleet, to a 'person of quality in Colchester', allegedly told of a force wracked by dissent and indecision at the highest level. He complained: 'Many here [are] turned cowards and fools, yet hanging on his Highness shamefully. We want money, that is the thing. The rogues begin to grumble for want.' He went on to make a depressing list of some of the time servers, using only their initials. 'I.P. is turned sot, R.H. frenzy, N.C. coward.' The main problem was the lack of any clear objective;

The Prince of VVales
His Coming to
YARMOUTH,
VVith 19. Saile of Shipping, & landing
an Armie for the Relief of
COLCHESTER.
Alſo a Fight between them and the Parliaments Forces; ſome of the Princes men taken Priſoners, and reſcued again by the town of *Yarmouth*, who joyne with the Prince, and keep out the Parliaments Forces.

WITH
A liſt of the Lords, Knights, and other Commanders come over with the Prince.

And Sir *Charles Lucas* his men roaſting a whole horſe, for joy of the Prince his coming.

Certified in a Letter from a Gentleman of Quality in the Army.

LONDON,
Printed by *Robert Auſtin*. July 27. 1647.[8]

41. The Prince of Wales was reported by some Royalist papers to have landed an invasion force at Great Yarmouth and was about to relieve Colchester. They soon had to back-track, however, when it became clear that the Prince had failed to get the local support he needed to carry through the scheme and was forced to sail away again without a fight. (Essex County Council)

the fleet seemed to be dawdling aimlessly up and down the coastline, wasting any real chance of making a difference to a Royalist war effort fast running out of steam. 'If we do not something speedily, or can land and have some join us, all is lost', he wrote. He then turned his rancour on would-be foreign allies, who were expected to support the British monarchy in its hour of need: 'Had not the drunken Dutch and the cowardly French deceived us, we had relieved you long since'.

The blow, such as it was when it finally fell, was aimed at the Norfolk port of Yarmouth. But it turned out to be an embarrassingly damp squib and only briefly disturbed the carefully preserved calm of a stubbornly neutral port. Some of the Prince's fleet drifted into the bay, sent a party ashore for provisions, took a group of worthies aboard the flagship to pay their respects to his Highness and then sailed away again. A demand that the town should yield to the King, caused momentary consternation and a crisis of loyalty among the corporation. Groping for a way to avoid any sort of commitment, they passed a resolution saying that 'it was contrary to the fundamental laws of the kingdom to give their assent for the letting in of a

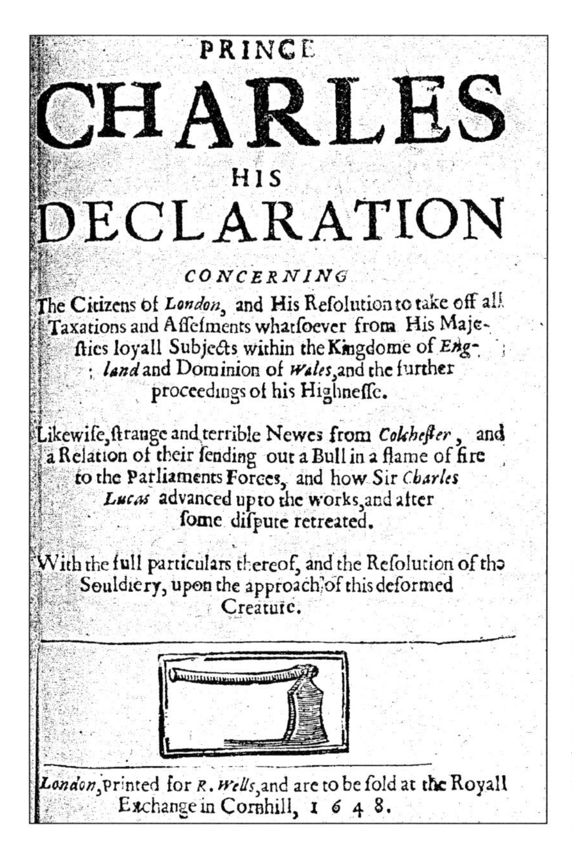

PRINCE
CHARLES
HIS
DECLARATION

CONCERNING

The Citizens of *London*, and His Reſolution to take off all Taxations and Aſſeſments whatſoever from His Majeſties loyall Subjects within the Kingdome of *England* and Dominion of *Wales*, and the further proceedings of his Highneſſe.

Likewiſe, ſtrange and terrible Newes from *Colcheſter*, and a Relation of their ſending out a Bull in a flame of fire to the Parliaments Forces, and how Sir *Charles Lucas* advanced up to the works, and after ſome diſpute retreated.

With the full particulars thereof, and the Reſolution of the Souldiery, upon the approach of this deformed Creature.

London, printed for *R. Wells*, and are to be ſold at the Royall Exchange in Cornhill, 1648.

42. Prince Charles promised to remove all wartime taxation and assessments 'from His Majesties loyall Subjects' if they helped return his father to the throne. However, he failed to use the ships under his command to fight what could have been a decisive battle with Parliament's navy in the Thames. (Essex County Council)

foreign enemy, saying that most of the Prince's forces were foreigners and strangers'. This produced some trouble on the streets from local Royalist factions who, 'perceiving the resolution of the Mayor and some of his brethren, resolved to frustrate their design, insomuch that there began a great insurrection within the town, [with] divers crying out "Hey for Prince Charles"'. Royalist newspapers made much of the municipal support for the Prince, estimating that the population were four to one in favour of welcoming him ashore; one report even said that 3,000–4,000 Royalist troops actually did land. The reality was far less dramatic.

The Royalist *Mercurius Melancholicus*, in a special edition on 31 July, had to correct its earlier optimistic bulletins, which had played up the scale of the trouble: 'The Prince did not himself land at Yarmouth (as was reported).' The paper was forced to add, by way of a rather lame explanation: 'The Prince's resolution is to gather the shipping together, the good effects whereof we doubt not but shortly to hear of.' Likewise, on 2 August *Mercurius Elencticus* also had to 'retract one error, committed the last week: and that was the landing of the Prince of Wales, at Yarmouth, which proved

... otherwise.' But the paper added with satisfaction that Yarmouth 'refused to give admittance to any of the Saints that were sent hither by the Army to prevent him'. Later, after the surrender of Colchester, Fairfax made immediately for Yarmouth to secure the town which, according to the *Kingdomes Weekly Intelligencer,* was still 'in a condition of neutrality'. It said that the port had been rather more willing 'to acknowledge than receive the Prince, and very unwilling to admit any garrison at all'. Yarmouth's determined struggle to avoid hostile entanglements of any kind was nothing unusual. Ever since the start of the Civil War in 1642, both Royalist and Parliamentary activists all over the country found that their support was inclined to melt away when people were faced with actually having to fight for their stated convictions. Many places, with varying degrees of success, tried to stick to the difficult path of armed neutrality: most however found themselves relentlessly forced to join one side or the other, or sometimes both in turn, as the fighting ebbed and flowed around them.

After the fiasco at Yarmouth, the Prince's navy drifted south into the mouth of the Thames, where the Earl of Warwick was effecting a rendezvous of all the units of the government navy which had remained loyal to Parliament. It was a job that required judgement and diplomacy because the allegiance of many ships was still in doubt, particularly those based at Portsmouth. The Prince had pledged to pardon and indemnify all Parliament men who changed sides, promising to pay the arrears owed to them. Charles had several options open to him when it came to using his new-found maritime power: he could harry shipping entering and leaving the Thames, putting commercial pressure on London to switch sides; he could attempt to induce a mutiny among the crews still loyal to Parliament; or, failing this, he could take on Warwick in battle on the Thames estuary hoping for a quick, decisive result. Some thought that he would make for the Isle of Wight to rescue his father from imprisonment. Fatally the Prince and his advisers once more dithered and late in August he decided to leave Lord Willoughby in charge and sail back to Holland alone. The decision caused near mutiny among his own men who, sensing the odds on their side, were all for fighting it out. The Prince was forced to turn his vessel around and rejoin the fleet. By that time gale force winds had sprung up making fighting impossible. Then the Royalist nerve failed at the last minute and they let slip their best opportunity ever for maritime victory. They failed to seize an opportunity to split the Parliamentary fleet in two and pick-off each section one at a time. Bitter recriminations followed; as they sailed back to Holland, one officer said 'I see no hope to reconcile our differences nor preserve this fleet'. The

Prince's indecision had allowed the Parliamentary navy to regroup and pursue him to Holland. There they bottled him up, under Dutch protection in the port of Helvoetsluys, until the following January, well after the Second Civil War had been decided and the King executed.

FISHING IN TROUBLED WATERS

The Prince of Wales's offer of amnesty, with all expenses paid, was issued from the deck of his rebel flagship and, he claimed, it had been received 'exceedingly well with many'. It was aimed not only at the waverers of the navy, but everyone on the Parliamentary side, soldiers, sailors and civilians. Specifically targeted were those with existing Royalist sympathies and the substantial number of moderate Presbyterians in the country 'who we hope will be ready to join [us], especially now the Scots are come in, who declare for the King, Covenant and Presbyterian government'. The Prince emphasised the message for them: 'We labour all we can to procure the union between Presbyterians and us'. The Parliament's propaganda machine was also targeting those who were actively considering quitting the cause and going over to the King. It quoted copiously from the Psalms: 'Put not your trust in princes, in the sons of man, in whom there is no help'. *Mercurius Britannicus* warned loyal Englishmen to beware of the intentions of the Cavaliers who, they said, 'fish in those troubled waters and hope to thrive by it'. They cautioned against accepting the word of:

> those scabbed gentlemen who would court you into their broken business and having performed it by your means, will trip up your heels and punish you for your old offences [for] which they will never forgive ye.

To prove the point the newspapers quoted at length from a letter allegedly sent by Sir Anthony St Leger, supposedly seized on its way from the Prince's fleet to Colchester: 'This letter was intercepted betwixt Deal and Sandown and the messenger apprehended'. In it the courtier was said to have roundly condemned all those who had ever opposed the royal cause promising them, despite all the pledges of amnesty, ultimate retribution: 'For all that have born arms for this corrupt Parliament, must hang, all; a fig for the treaty'. And for the Royalists, still shut up in Colchester, there was this grim message: 'As for those that cowardly left you, they will be hanged as well as the Independents and Roundheads; take notice of all that ran from you.' This attitude apparently applied to everyone ever tainted with Parliamentary connections. The seamen who had mutinied against Parliament for the King were allegedly on the hit-list: 'We know not how to trust the turn-coat mariners, his Highness will never forget their forwardness to assist the Parliament first. We will pay them at last.' But in the meantime, as cynically straightforward as it was, the advice was clear: 'Promise them land, offices, anything for our design.' Whether this letter was genuine, or only existed in the vivid imagination of a creative propagandist, it voiced the suspicions of many sceptics: 'Therefore beware, O Englishmen, of any further engagement and lay hold of the Parliament's clemency in time.'

On the front-line at Colchester a relentless psychological war was being waged, particularly by the Parliamentarian forces. Carter noted that the enemy spread

> strange and improbable news of great victories over the Scots long before they ever received them, and [issued] lists of prisoners who were taken never in arms, and such like whimsies, hoping thereby to terrify the inferior sort of soldiers and bring them to a timorous apprehension of their condition.

In an effort to foment mutiny in the Royalist ranks 'to force their officers to treat for conditions, or leave them in the lurch', the army sent 'private papers into the town incensing the soldiers against their officers, reproaching them with the odious name of rebels'. At one point they took to firing arrows over the walls offering amnesty to the rank and file of the garrison with 'liberty to go to their own homes without plunder'. According to Carter this produced the opposite of the desired reaction, stiffening rather than weakening the troops' resolve to 'either live with liberty or die with honour, neither of which could arise by a poor submission to an ignoble enemy'. On 11 August he reported that more propaganda arrows were fired over the defences which his men 'resolved to answer'. They took their own arrows, said Carter (coyly sparing his readers' blushes), and after they had 'anointed them with a t...d' sent them back with: 'an answer from Colchester, 11 August 1648, as you may smell.'

There was little sympathy for the civilians of Colchester trapped in their stricken town by the ill-fortunes of war. According to the Parliamentary press, they were far from innocent victims but rather the authors of their own misfortune by opening their gates to the Earl of Norwich. 'The Lord bring the hearts of that people in and about the town to a true sight of the cause whereof this great wrath is come upon them', cried the writer of *Colchester Teares*. 'The immediate cause of Jerusalem's ruin was the mocking of the messengers of God, despising his word and misusing his prophets, till their was no remedy.' Colchester, he concluded, must now serve as an example to all those places which might be lured, for whatever reason, from the godly path: 'we humbly hope and pray that all moderate men will a little look into, and by the sad example of mournful and much-lamented Colchester, take warning in time.' An officer in Fairfax's army added bluntly: 'Let this be a warning to London.' The rhetoric of terror was also used to demoralise the defiant town itself: 'Colchester shall be cast into the jaws of a victorious and enraged soldiery', boomed *Mercurius Bellicus*, 'and speedily you will then perceive whether it had not been better to have kept the British ocean between you and the fire, than have leapt into it with more danger to yourselves than trouble to any other.'

The propaganda sometimes took some surreal twists. At the end of July it was reported that a 'flaming bull' had been released from behind the town's defences. Sir Charles Lucas, looking for a 'miraculous stratagem' to spread dread among the ranks of the enemy, had fitted the poor animal with a coat of thinly beaten lead, over which was poured flax, tar and pitch. This was then set alight and the bull sent bellowing in terror and pain towards the leaguer, followed by some of his attack troops. Startled by 'the hideous noise of this deformed beast' some in the leaguer 'cried out the Devil was coming [but] others stood to it and resolved to fight him was he never so monstrous'. The burning bull was turned around in mid-charge by a volley of muskets and proceeded to cause consternation among those who had released him doing 'execution upon his masters who also retreated'. The Royalists claimed that they had killed some 500 men with this trick, but the Parliamentary press rubbished this, saying the claim carried about as much credence as the rumours of the 'Prince's landing and raising the Siege of Colchester'.

On its side the army appeared to be resorting to astrology to shape strategy. It was reported that in mid-July they were so frustrated by the lack of progress at Colchester that they had sought the advice of two astrologers of high repute, William Lilly and John Booker. Such was their reputation that their arrival in the leaguer provoked a flurry of printed reaction. 'Prophetical Quacks', screamed *Mercurius Bellicus*, 'mere gypsies, ignorant (but cunning in Knavery) to delude the poor people out of their pence.'

They were 'conjuring the figures and characters', said the *Parliament Kite*, 'and yet can find no sign of Parliament's recovery.' As a result the paper conjectured that MPs would: 'Vote the stars enemies and traitors to the Parliament and Kingdom, and so sequester and sell the twelve houses of the heavens, and bestow them on Lilly and Booker for a gratuity for their good counsel.' *Mercurius Britannicus* was quick to jump to the astrologers' defence: 'thou presume to jibe yet be confident their skills in the art they profess is such as we may well expect an event answerable to their predictions [i.e. a Parliamentary victory].' But as July turned into August no-one, other than an astrologer, would have presumed to forecast defeat for the King's caused Parliament still faced wide-ranging military opposition in several scattered theatres of operation, including the North where a Scots army was now encamped on English soil.

PRESTON

On 8 July the Scots army of Engagement, under the command of the Duke of Hamilton, had finally managed to recruit enough troops to begin its march south of the border. Raising the necessary numbers had taken an inordinate length of time because of deep divisions in the Covenanting movement. Strong opposition to any form of alliance with Charles Stuart had come from the godly Covenanters of the Kirk. As described in chapter 3, their active campaigning against the whole venture meant that the Engagers collected only a third of the total they originally wanted. But by the end of June Sir Marmaduke Langdale, who had been penned in at Carlisle by Major-General Lambert, was sending constant appeals for help to Scotland. Both he and the garrison at Colchester were now relying on intervention from the north. When Hamilton eventually responded it was with a force of 9,000 men, most of them raw recruits, who were badly provisioned, and lacking artillery, ammunition and adequate numbers of cavalry. Yet their numbers still forced Lambert to fight a series of tactical withdrawals to a safe distance there to await the arrival of Cromwell and his reinforcements. But Hamilton, instead of moving quickly to exploit the New Model Army's weakness in numbers and bring prompt aid to the rest of the English rebels, decided to play a cautious game. He stayed put and waited for the rest of his army to catch up with him. The entire and vital month of July was wasted as Hamilton's fatal indecision seemed to turn to total paralysis. Nothing at all happened, except that his idle and poorly supplied army alienated the whole population of the border country by plundering their homes, driving off entire herds of animals and even kidnapping children and ransoming them to their parents at swordpoint. Many residents of Cumberland and Westmoreland became refugees in neighbouring counties. Resentment grew as the Scots made a name for themselves as nothing more than brutal invaders – and this in a normally Royalist-inclined neighbourhood.

Hamilton's inaction meant that he failed to bring the New Model Army to battle while he heavily outnumbered them and before they were able to make a junction with Cromwell's reinforcements, marching north from Wales, as fast as their legs would carry them. By 8 August Cromwell had arrived. He and Lambert reviewed their combined force together near Leeds. Hamilton finally decided he was ready to move south on 14 August, choosing a route through Lancashire in the hope of picking up more Royalist support that way. Fatally he allowed his cavalry to move on ahead by at least sixteen miles, leaving the bulk of his men vulnerably strung out. To make matters worse his intelligence was so bad that when he reached Preston he had no idea where Cromwell was. By the time the full, awful truth dawned on him, Langdale's army and a large part of his own, had been almost wiped out. A running battle ensued with the remainder of the Scots all the way to Winwick, near Warrington, where, two days later, they too were overwhelmed. The Engagers' army had been annihilated by 19 August. A combination of circumstances had doomed the enterprise: support at home for them was weak and the delay in raising an army at all proved fatal when it came to coordinating with the English rebels; Hamilton's indecision, once he had arrived in England, compounded the problems; he failed to formulate a decisive plan of action and allowed Cromwell not only to rendezvous with Lambert's force, but to catch him in the open with his army strung out a day's march apart; he was dogged all the way by indiscipline and insubordination from quarrelsome officers more preoccupied with their own vendettas than invading England. Cromwell commanded his much smaller, but infinitely more dedicated army, with his usual genius, skill and daring. He lost only 100 men during three days of action, which saw thousands of Scots slaughtered. His exhausted troops still managed to find the energy to chase the Scots remnants into the Midlands, capturing Hamilton at Uttoxeter and Langdale at an alehouse near Nottingham.

The battle of Preston was effectively the end of the King's hopes of a military victory and it was also the beginning of the end of Colchester's long

43. Oliver Cromwell: once more his military genius, together with the total commitment and discipline of the men of the New Model Army, crushed a much larger combined force of Scotsmen and Royalist rebels at the battle of Preston. The victory spelt the beginning of the end for the garrison at Colchester.

agony. 'Surely', wrote Cromwell in his first report to Parliament after the victory, 'this is nothing but the hand of God'. He then rode north to provide the military muscle for a coup by the godly party of the Kirk, who in January 1649 excluded all Engagers from civil office and, for the time being at least, secured the English Parliament's backdoor against further hostile intervention.

MUTINY

The devastating news of Cromwell's victory at Preston was delivered to the garrison at Colchester on 24 August. 'The enemy sent a paper kite into the town', Carter recalled, 'which hovered for a good while over it [before] they let it drop.' It carried the 'revelation of a great victory over the Scots and their general rout'. In the next few hours 'they made a general triumph through the whole leaguer, giving a volley of both small and great shot, which gave alarm that an all out assault was starting'. Of course everyone knew that Fairfax's 'best policy was to forebear' and: by this time he was required to do absolutely nothing to win. Carter said that the army 'had drawn their approaches so near the line under Berry Fields, by the shelter of the wall, that the soldiers from their trenches and ours might talk together and throw stones at one another, both of which they frequently did'.

For many of the defenders throwing stones was the best they could do. For a week now the high command knew that their magazine could 'not maintain two hours fight if a storm should happen'. The town had been

> plunged into very great extremities ... We had scarce left uneaten one cat or dog some horses we had yet alive, but not many ... there was no corn left for one day's provision our hopes were now dissolved into absolute fear and unavoidable ruin.

A council of war had agreed said Carter 'that it was the best course to treat with the enemy. We had done our utmost and were at last destitute of any relief'. On 17 August a local doctor was sent to see what concessions could be obtained and returned with the same old news that only 'inferior officers and soldiers' would be guaranteed free quarter. Senior officers would have to 'submit to mercy' – an unpredictable fate in the current circumstances, which could mean the exact opposite happening. Nothing had changed and according to Carter, 'we were not resolved to surrender on those dishonourable terms'. This news caused near riot among the starving civilians. Their plight was very much worse in most cases than the troops and it widened the rift between them and the military, who were now frequently criticised for their callous disregard for the local population. One Royalist officer, it was said, told a woman begging food for her starving baby: 'God Damn me, that child would make a good deal of meat well boiled'. The same woman had already told the soldiers that 'could they get dogs and cats to eat, it would be happy for them'. The Colchester diarist, noted that when news leaked out that the Royalist command were planning to fight on 'the people came about them again [at headquarters] for bread'. Norwich responded by 'setting open the gates and bid them go out to the enemy, which a great many did willingly'. The earl also 'ordered all the rest that came about his door to be turned out after them'. It was a welcome development for him. The previous day he had considered forcibly expelling 'all such inhabitants within this town as have no provisions for the maintenance of themselves and families', but he soon realised that this would cause more trouble than it would solve. Now the townspeople seemed to have answered the problem for him. However, the scenes which followed in no-man's-land were extremely brutal and harrowing.

Units of the army under the command of Colonel Rainsborough – back in soldiers uniform after his abortive attempt to run the navy – had been given orders that the civilians, whatever their state, should not be allowed to leave the town. He was told to open fire, if necessary, to stop them: Carter called it an 'unchristian, though politic order'. The army secretary Rushworth logged what happened next: 'five hundred women and children, marched with much confidence toward Colonel Rainsborough's quarters'. His immediate reaction was to order 'a cannon to be shot off, but so as not to hurt them [but] they came on not withstanding. He [then] orders the firing of some muskets with powder [blanks] that daunts them not.' Reporting the incident the *Kingdomes Weekly Intelligencer*, said that 'so sad [was] their condition then, that rather than return to the town they adventured on the mercy of the cannon and did run up to the very mouth of it.' Colonel Rainsborough then ordered his troops to strip those women who refused to budge, 'the fear and shame whereof caused the women to go back, and their sad children with them'. By this time however, the garrison, obviously glad to be rid of these extra mouths to feed, refused to take them back, leaving them stranded between the lines: 'They would not be admitted into the town again, the gates and all the avenues being made fast, whereupon they were enforced to take unto a mill for their protection'. The civilians were only allowed back into town after Fairfax himself threatened to put the entire garrison to the sword if they weren't.

On 23 August the officers and gentlemen of the garrison had signed an agreement 'ourselves not to desert each other, nor the foot soldiers, till we have forced our passage through all that shall oppose us, or perish in the act'. The following day the shock news from Preston arrived, but after the initial impact the garrison declared they were still ready to dispute the town street by street whatever the cost. They even kept 'iron pots and cauldrons of scalding pitch' on the boil 'to cast over the ramparts upon them had they began their storm'. By 25 August plans for a suicide breakout by the entire garrison were finalised. The Colchester diarist noted that they had 'resolved to die with their swords in their hands rather than yield'. Carter explained:

> Considering the melancholy condition we were plunged into, through the defeat of the Scots, the disloyalty of the whole kingdom and the want we were of provision to subsist, it was the final resolution of the council of war to draw out the whole party that night, both horse and foot, with what ammunition was left ... to set open the gates and march out and storm their line or perish in the attempt.

All 'bag or baggage' was to be left behind: 'If we failed of a certainty we should have no need of them'. Carter agreed that it was 'a desperate mission, but must be deemed noble'. If it succeeded they would win 'not only their liberty, but the freedom and peace of the whole kingdom'. He recalled that other historically hopeless gambles had succeeded in he past, but such death-or-glory fantasies were a little too much for the long suffering troops and they mutinied.

The night before the breakout Carter reported that:

> some mutinous spirit had insinuated into the private soldiers that the officers and the rest of the gentlemen were resolved to break through the leaguer and escape, leaving them all to shift for themselves.

This would have been disastrous for them: Fairfax, if provoked, could cancel his offer of amnesty at any time and butcher them all instead, as happened with regularity on the continent. The 'spark rose to such a flame', said Carter, '[that] those soldiers, so remarkably gallant before ... hurried into a frenzy of desperate mutiny.' It spread like wildfire around the entire Colchester perimeter: 'In some parts they threatened to cast their officers over the line.' Before dawn 'so high was the mutiny grown' that it was obvious that it would end 'in immediate ruin for themselves and their officers'. On the other side the army were well aware of the precarious position of the Royalist high command; they were being informed daily by those 'incendiaries among us [who gave] the enemy notice that they might make the best use of it'. This was the end of resistance: 'The soldiers, till then, never having acted anything dishonourable, or like the most gallant fellows ... never showing the least discontent at any orders which were given.' They had finally had enough.

Norwich was left with little option but to tell his men that their officers were prepared to 'deliver themselves up as prisoners to the enemy, if thereby they could purchase them an honourable liberty'. As final articles of surrender were being drawn up on 27 August Carter complained that 'the enemy's army and ours were already mixed in many places of the line and no fire given on either side, as if we had been prisoners long before any conclusion was made'. Colonel Samuel Tuke was dispatched to Fairfax's headquarters with full powers to conclude conditions: 'there was no refuge, no remedy left, nor anything to trust to, but what conditions the enemy would give us.' The garrison had only one and a half barrels of gunpowder left.

SURRENDER

By the end of the day on 27 August, nine articles of surrender were drawn up between the negotiators of both sides. It was agreed that by eight o' clock the following morning 'all guards within the town of Colchester shall be withdrawn from the line'; at nine o' clock all the horses that had survived, together with all saddles and bridles, were to be left in St Mary's churchyard; one hour later, at ten o' clock, 'all the arms, colours and drums belonging to any person in Colchester' were to be brought to St James's Church 'and delivered without wilful spoil or embezzlement'; all ammunition was to be 'preserved in the places where it lies' and all the big guns left 'at the several platforms and places where they are now planted'. The army guaranteed that the sick and wounded would not be moved, being 'kept and provided for with accommodation requisite for men in their condition until they recovered'. The surrender of 'all private soldiers and officers under captain', with all their clothes and baggage, was to be taken at ten o' clock in the Fryer's Yard, adjoining East Gate, where 'they shall have fair quarter'. At eleven o' clock the 'Lords and all captains and superior officers and

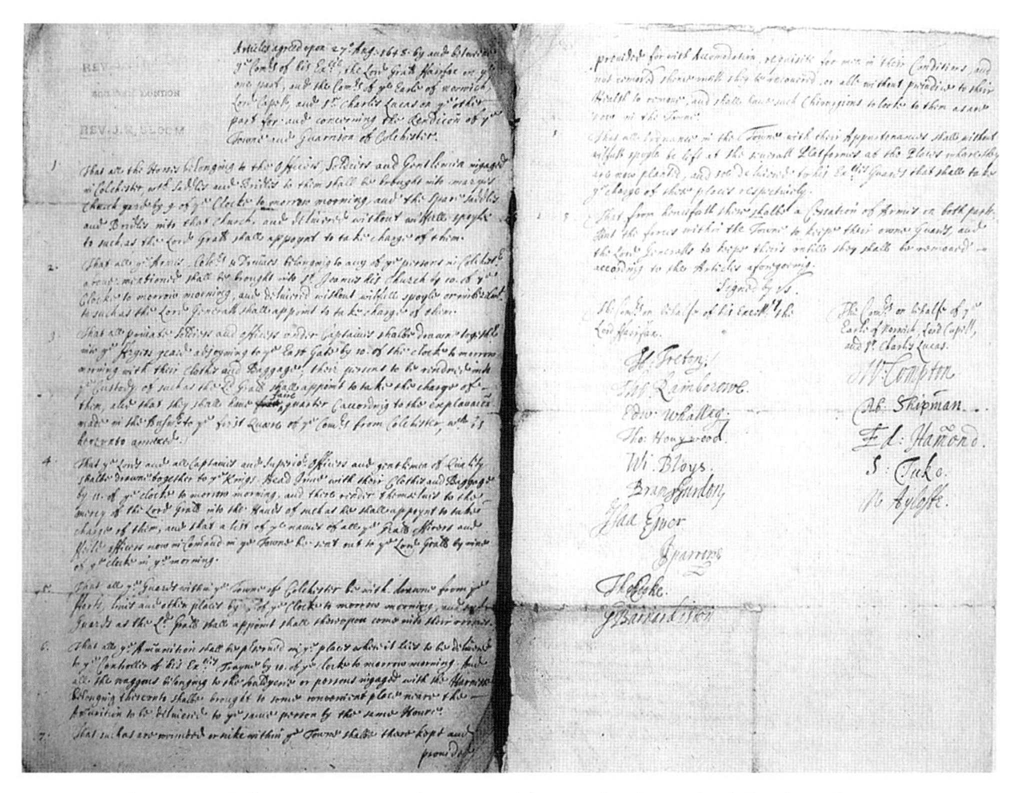

44. The original document surrendering Colchester: by the end of the day of 27 August nine articles of surrender had been drawn up for the belligerents to sign. The surrender of the town was taken the following morning, seventy-five days after the start of the siege. (Colchester Museums)

gentlemen of distinction shall be drawn together to the King's Head and there submit themselves to the mercy of the Lord General'.

Immediately two contentious questions came up – portentous in the light of subsequent events: what was 'fair quarter' and 'what is meant by rendering to mercy?' They were to fuel a controversy which surrounded the surrender forever afterwards. Fair quarter was spelled out as being 'free from wounding, or beating, shall enjoy warm clothes to cover them [and] shall be maintained with victuals fit for prisoners, whilst they shall be kept prisoners'. Rendering 'to mercy', it was understood, was submitting 'without certain assurance of quarter, so as the Lord General may be free to put some immediately to the sword (if he see cause)'. However the following assurance was added: 'his excellency [Fairfax] intends chiefly, and for the generality of those under that condition, to surrender them to mercy of the Parliament.' Fairfax, it was stated, had never 'given cause to doubt his civility' towards prisoners in the past, but ominously a get-out clause was

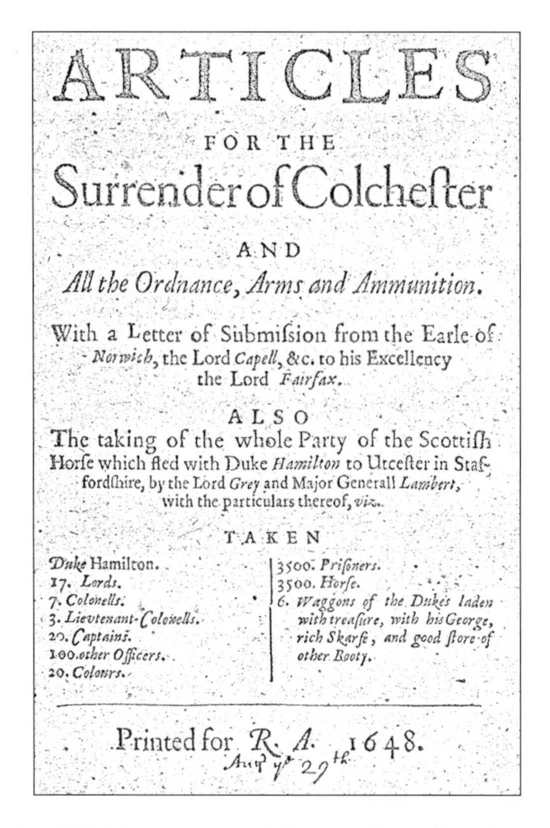

ARTICLES

FOR THE

Surrender of Colcheſter

AND

All the Ordnance, Arms and Ammunition.

With a Letter of Submiſsion from the Earle of *Norwich*, the Lord *Capell*, &c. to his Excellency the Lord *Fairfax*.

ALSO

The taking of the whole Party of the Scottiſh Horſe which fled with Duke *Hamilton* to Utceſter in Staffordſhire, by the Lord *Grey* and Major Generall *Lambert*, with the particulars thereof, *viz.*

TAKEN

Duke Hamilton.	3500. *Priſoners.*
17. *Lords.*	3500. *Horſe.*
7. *Colonells.*	6. *Waggons of the Dukes laden with treaſure, with his George, rich Skarfe, and good ſtore of other Booty.*
3. *Lievtenant-Colonells.*	
20. *Captains.*	
100. *other Officers.*	
20. *Colours.*	

Printed for *R. A.* 1648.

45. The surrender of Colchester removed the most immediate threat to London and effectively marked the end of the Second Civil War. This pamphlet gives details of the terms, which the Royalists immediately accused Parliament of breaching. Also here is reported the capture, in Staffordshire, of the Duke of Hamilton who led the doomed invasion from Scotland on behalf of the King. (Essex County Council)

added: 'by their being rendered to mercy he stands not engaged thereby'.

Carter calculated that a total of 3,530 men had survived to surrender, of which 3,067 were 'private soldiers'. Some 2,000 of the garrison had died. No-one calculated the full death toll among civilians and troops – of all those 'killed in the siege and dead of the flux and other distempers occasioned by bad diet, which were very many'. However, it was the brutal treatment then meted out to the rank and file troops, and the even greater outrage provoked by the summary execution of the two senior officers responsible for the defence, Sir Charles Lucas and Sir George Lisle, that was to shock a nation already hardened by years of brutal civil war. This violent aftermath was to cast a long shadow over the otherwise humanitarian reputation of Sir Thomas Fairfax, commander-in-chief of the New Model Army.

6

CONTRARY TO THE RULES OF HONOUR

At two o' clock on the afternoon of 28 August, seventy-five days after he had ridden up with the advance units of his cavalry, Sir Thomas Fairfax entered Colchester. He made no effort to talk to either his aristocratic prisoners or any of their senior Royalist officers. It appeared that he wanted only to satisfy his curiosity about the nature of the defences which had for so long stood in his way. The army's secretary, John Rushworth, who accompanied him, was impressed: 'we rode round about the wall of the town and found it a very strong place in all parts of it. Where it was weakest there they [had] made strong works and strengthened it with earth.' Quartermaster General Carter, now a prisoner of war, said that the General 'found just cause for admiration and wondered how it was possible we could maintain it so long against him, whose very name, as he thought, was enough to conquer'. For two and a half months they had held out against the New Model Army, forcing its lengthy commitment to a siege of campaign proportions. The size of the ensuing operation awed those who saw it as well as those who took part. One Parliamentary officer observed on the day of surrender: 'The like line, regular works, fortifications and approaches have not been made in any part of the kingdom since the wars began.'

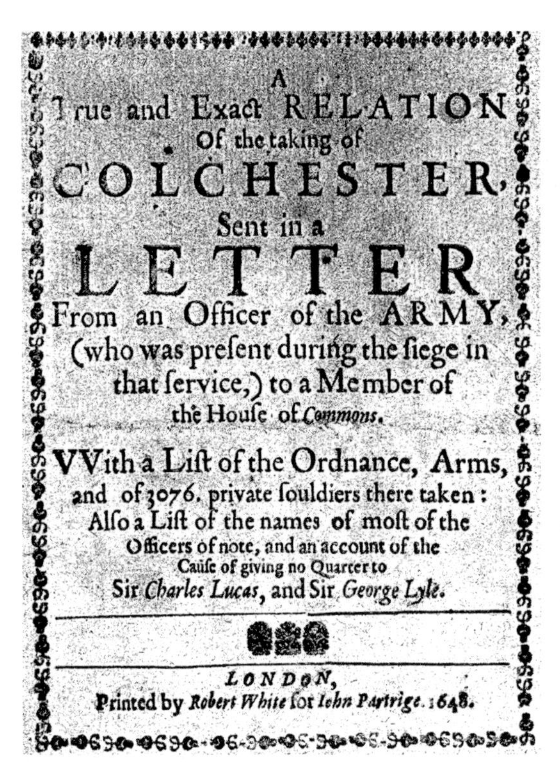
A
True and Exact RELATION
Of the taking of
COLCHESTER,
Sent in a
LETTER
From an Officer of the ARMY,
(who was present during the siege in
that service,) to a Member of
the House of *Commons*.

VVith a List of the Ordnance, Arms,
and of 3076. private souldiers there taken:
Also a List of the names of most of the
Officers of note, and an account of the
Cause of giving no Quarter to
Sir *Charles Lucas*, and Sir *George Lyle*.

LONDON,
Printed by *Robert White* for *Iohn Partrige*. 1648.

46. The siege of Colchester seen through the eyes of a serving officer: this pamphlet contained a description of the appalling state of the town and its inhabitants immediately upon surrender. Fairfax's first action was to examine in person the earthworks and the defences which had withstood his siege for such a long time. (Essex County Council)

The town itself was a 'sad spectacle', many of its houses reduced to rubble and ashes and its 'famished' inhabitants so 'sickly and weak' that they were forced to fight over the last scraps of animal fodder 'for the preservation of life'. The *Moderate* reported: 'Inhabitants who lived about three months since in good quality' were now reduced to begging from the victors, while 'others, ashamed to beg, do almost perish for want of sustenance'. Another officer from the leaguer described what he saw of the aftermath: 'The town hath suffered as well as the men. They who had houses to live in now live desolate for want of habitation.' But there was little pity for the victims 'since they traded with Cavaliers'. The mayor had petitioned Fairfax asking that what remained of his 'miserable, decayed and wasted town' should be spared plunder by the incoming troops. It was, but only after an enormous fine of £14,000 had been agreed by way of compensation, something in the region of £2 million at today's prices.

Shortly after the inspection, however, Fairfax called a council of war 'according to his appointment'. It was these men who Carter alleged 'luxuriated their insatiable malice in a collation of loyal blood and decreed the barbarous sacrifice of innocent virtue'. They ordered the immediate execution of Lucas and Lisle. The first premonitions of what was in store

47. The Old King's Head, now a solicitor's office, where the Royalist leaders and their senior officers were held after surrendering.

came at the King's Head, where the senior officers were being held: it is now a solicitor's office just off Head Street. Carter recalled:

> They sent Colonel Ewers to the King's Head to visit, as we thought, the lords and gentlemen, but he brought a sentence of death in his heart, though not immediately in his mouth, which easily discovered itself in his death-like countenance.

He first saluted the Earl of Norwich, Lord Capel and Lord Loughborough, then turning to Sir Charles Lucas, 'with a slighting gesture', told him that 'the General desired to speak to him [and] Sir George Lisle, Sir Bernard Gascoigne and Colonel Farre'. The only one of the group missing was Farre. Fortunately for him, he had managed to escape in the confusion of the surrender. Although he was recaptured soon afterwards, he had, by being absent at the vital time, saved his skin. Lucas, 'presaging what indeed afterwards followed, took his solemn leave of the lords and the rest of his fellow prisoners'.

48. Sir Bernard Gascoigne: he was to have faced the firing squad, along with Sir Charles Lucas and Sir George Lisle. At the last moment it was discovered that he was an Italian. His real name was Bernardo Guasconi and he had friends in high places in the court of Tuscany. It was thought to be wiser, diplomatically, to spare his life. (Colchester Museums)

TRAITORS AND REBELS

The trio were brought before the army's council of war sitting in the Town Hall. Henry Ireton not Fairfax presided; significantly the Lord General was not even present. The prisoners had anyway been tried in their absence. They were told: 'That after so long and obstinate a defence, it was highly necessary, for the example of others, that some military justice be executed'. Lucas and Lisle were to be 'immediately shot to death', as was Sir Bernard Gascoigne, another professional soldier – a 'soldier of fortune', as all three were later contemptuously described. Gascoigne he said was an Italian – his real name was Bernardo Guasconi – a man with influential friends in Tuscany, including the Grand-Duke himself. He enjoyed a colourful reputation across the continent as a swashbuckling soldier and diplomat and was, like Lucas and Lisle, a veteran of the European wars. He also had close royal connections in England and had been commissioned by the King in 1644. What earned him a death sentence now was that he, with the other professionals, was considered to have played a prominent part in the prolonged defence of Colchester, commanding, with panache, a regiment of horse. According to Carter, he was mistaken for an English gentleman and a knight of the realm 'that they might sacrifice three of that rank'. Gascoigne managed to escape execution at the eleventh hour only after the extent of his personal ties to the court in Florence became clear.

From the Town Hall the three men were marched to the castle, which also served as the county gaol, and told to prepare for death. Here Lucas insisted to all present that: 'In order to do my duty, I came to this place in the Prince's service, but since I came hither I am not guilty of wronging the least person, the least soldier in this army. I die for my prince.' It was, however, the arrival on the scene of Colonel Henry Ireton, Cromwell's radical son-in-law and one of the principal army commanders at the siege, which provoked a verbal exchange which was to sum up succinctly what the Second Civil War had been all about. In his detailed account of the conversation William Clarke, secretary of the army, recorded that Sir Charles asked Ireton: 'by whom am I condemned, whether by my Lord Fairfax alone, or by the council of war. I beseech you to let me know my judge.' Ireton told him:

> I may answer so far, as you are condemned by the Parliament upon your own actions. [The war] wherein you have so voluntarily a second time engaged, hath rendered you, in their judgement [and]... your whole party, deserving death.

49. Colchester Castle: it was used as the county gaol at the time of the siege and Lucas and Lisle were housed here before being marched out to their execution. It was in their cell that Lucas argued with Henry Ireton about the nature of treachery and loyalty.

And he went on: 'Know yourself, as all others that engage a second time against the Parliament, are traitors and rebels, and they do employ us, as soldiers by authority from them, to suppress and destroy ... Our commission, it is that'. They had surrendered, said Ireton, with 'no assurance of quarter' and the General was perfectly at liberty to 'to put some of you to the sword, if he saw cause'.

'Sir', replied Lucas,

> this is a very nice point to take away a man's life when there is a law in the kingdom and look to it lest my blood be upon you. I do plead before you all the laws of the kingdom. I have fought with a commission from those who were my sovereigns.

Ireton tried to bring the arguments to a close: 'Sir, we have nothing more to add to that.' But he could not resist making a final point: 'had not you by arms stopped the laws of the land?'

Still Lucas argued that this amounted to an unprecedented military lynching: 'It was never known that men were killed in cold blood before', – by which he presumably meant gentlemen. It was at this point that two soldiers standing nearby spoke up. They maintained that Lucas had in fact done that very thing in the First Civil War at Stinchcombe in Gloucestershire when between twenty and forty men of a Parliamentary garrison were put to the sword.

Ireton attempted once more to end the debate: 'You being a traitor...' but at this point a furious Sir Charles broke in and loudly proclaimed: 'I am no traitor, but a true English subject of my King and the laws of the kingdom. Sir you ought to prove me one before you condemn me to be a traitor.'

Ireton tried again: 'We tell you what judgement you are concluded by, and that is by the judgement of Parliament.'

Sir Charles: 'I can say no more. I shall only desire that my life may satisfy for all the rest of these gentlemen and these gentlemen may go free.' According to Carter, Lucas added a further point: 'Alas you deceive yourselves, me you cannot. We are conquered and must be what you please to make us.' He then went to his death 'as cheerful as one going to a banquet'.

EXECUTION

The firing squad was drawn up in front of the grim, north wall of Colchester Castle, at a 'green spot of ground'. Lucas was the first to face them. Secretary Clarke recorded his final words: 'Remember me to all my friends and tell them that I have died in a good cause. If I have offended any, I desire their forgiveness'. He then requested a 'decent burial' with his ancestors and, recalling the earlier desecration of the family crypt by Parliamentary soldiers, added: 'Let us from henceforth lie in quiet'. Clarke's account of Sir Charles's final moments is matter-of-fact: on his uttering 'Oh Father, Son and Holy Ghost, receive my soul', six dragoons 'with fire locks, discharged at him and after his falling, Sir George Lisle, having kissed him, was also shot to death'.

Carter's account is naturally more flamboyant: three of Fairfax's most senior commanders, Ireton, Rainsborough and Whalley, watched as Sir Charles 'with a cheerful countenance, opened his doublet and showed them his breast; and then placing his hands by his side, called out to his executioners, "See I am ready for you. And now rebels, do your worst."' Next came Sir George Lisle. Brought from a short distance away, he first knelt by

50. Sir Charles Lucas and Sir George Lisle became instant martyrs for the Royalist cause after their summary trial and execution. Pamphlets like this sang their praises, giving several versions of their last words. This one attributes to Lucas the enduring couplet: 'Your shot your shame,/Our fall, our fame'. (Colchester County Museums)

51. Lucas and Lisle were shot against this, the north wall of the castle, where a memorial to their execution stands to this day. For many years it was said that the grass refused to grow at the spot, although sceptics put this story down to the excesses of the tourist trade, which quickly flourished afterwards.

his fallen friend, and then 'took out of his pocket five gold pieces, which was all the money he had about him'. He gave the firing squad one and instructed his servant, who stood nearby, to take the other four to friends in London as 'his last legacy.' He then complained to the witnesses: 'How many of your lives who are now present here, have I saved in hot blood and must now myself be most barbarously murdered in cold.' Lisle turned to face the firing squad and invited them to step a little closer to get a better shot. 'I'll warrant ye, sir, we'll hit you', said one, at which Sir George smiled grimly and replied: 'I have been nearer you when you missed me.' After kneeling in prayer he added: 'I am now ready; traitors do your worst.'

Sir Bernard Gascoigne was due for execution next. He had 'served the King in the war and afterwards remained in London, till the unhappy adventure of Colchester and then accompanied his friends thither'. Carter recalled that Gascoigne first asked for 'pen ink and paper, that he might write a letter to his prince, the great Duke [of Tuscany] that his Highness might know in what manner he lost his life'. He wanted to ensure, he said, that 'his heirs might possess his estate'. It was only after these requests were passed on to the senior men present, and 'after a consultation held', was Sir Bernard 'ordered to be brought back and kept with the prisoners'. According to Carter, after further discussion among the council of war they decided 'that if they took away the life of a foreigner, who seemed to be a person of quality, their friends, or children, who should visit Italy might pay dear for many generations'.

Among the aristocratic prisoners, the leaders of the revolt, the news of the executions, brought to them by Fairfax himself, caused much anger. The ageing Earl of Norwich, nominally the head of the insurrection, and Lord Capel the soldier-peer and militant Royalist, were assured by Fairfax that their lives, at least for the time being, 'were safe and they should be well treated and disposed of as Parliament should direct'. Lord Capel, bristling with indignation, told Fairfax, that 'the General should have received their thanks if he had saved the lives of those two worthy knights ... which they valued more than their own'. Their lordships, he said, had 'acted alike in the engagement and management of the whole affair [and] they should have shared one fate'. He added that Fairfax and his officers 'would do well to finish their work by executing the same rigour on the rest'. Carter noted that 'this answer was very displeasing to Fairfax and the other officers', particularly to Ireton, who he blamed for all that had happened. It was Ireton, he said, who 'swayed the General and was upon all occasions of an unmerciful and bloody nature'. In fact Carter was convinced that it was this outburst from Capel, which later sealed his fate and sent him to the block, when the more pliant Norwich managed to escape the same fate, albeit by only a hair's breadth.

The following day, in his report to the Earl of Manchester the Speaker of the House of Lords, Fairfax explained his actions. This terse account was the fullest he ever gave about the incident:

> seeing that for some satisfaction to military justice, and in part to avenge for the innocent blood they have caused to be spilt and the trouble, damage and mischief that they have brought upon the town, this country and the kingdom, I have, with the advice of the council of war, ... ordered two of them, who were rendered to mercy, to be shot to death before any of them had quarter assured them. The persons pitched upon for this example were Sir Charles Lucas and Sir George Lisle, in whose military execution I hope your Lordships will not find cause to think your honour or justice prejudiced. As for the Lord Goring [Earl of Norwich], Lord Capel

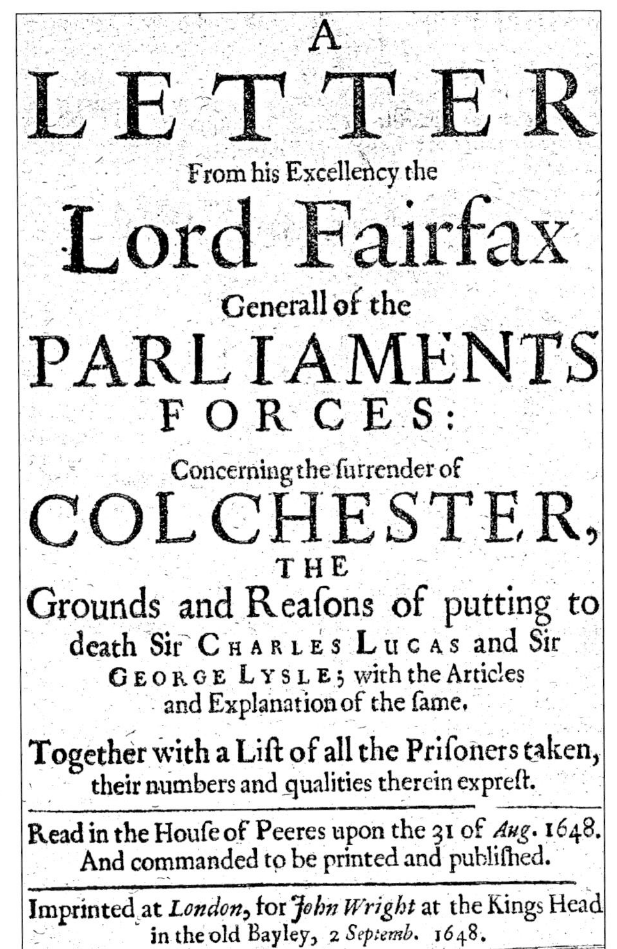
A
LETTER
From his Excellency the
Lord Fairfax
Generall of the
PARLIAMENTS
FORCES:
Concerning the ſurrender of
COLCHESTER,
THE
Grounds and Reaſons of putting to
death Sir CHARLES LUCAS and Sir
GEORGE LYSLE; with the Articles
and Explanation of the ſame.
Together with a Liſt of all the Priſoners taken,
their numbers and qualities therein expreſt.

Read in the Houſe of Peeres upon the 31 of *Aug*. 1648.
And commanded to be printed and publiſhed.

Imprinted at *London*, for *John Wright* at the Kings Head
in the old Bayley, 2 *Septemb*. 1648.

52. Here Sir Thomas Fairfax explains to Parliament why he had Lucas and Lisle executed. They were 'pitched upon' as an example to others for the 'mischief they had brought upon the town' and to avenge all 'the innocent blood they have caused to be split'. He said that he was perfectly entitled, by the rules of war, to have them shot. (Essex County Council)

> and the rest of the persons now assured of quarter I do render to Parliament's judgement for further public justice and mercy, to be used as you shall see cause.

Only some years later did Fairfax mention the incident again and then only briefly, in a characteristically 'Short Memorial' of his career: Lisle and Lucas, he said were 'soldiers of fortune and, falling into our hands by chance of war, were executed'.

The post-mortem of history, the labelling of heroes and villains, began almost as soon as the last echoes of the firing squad had reverberated from the grey stone walls of Colchester Castle. Pro-army pamphlets defended the executions, condemning Sir Charles as 'the cause of the ruin of the place, his interest in the town drawing the army thither ... He was the head of all those that did rise in this county'. But it was the royal propagandists who enjoyed a real field day.

MARTYRDOM

The controversy began almost immediately in the House of Commons, where daily members were growing more sympathetic to the King and suspicious of the increasingly hardline tendencies of the army. Some MPs were outraged; the executions were 'without precedent', they said, and 'he [Lucas] ought to have been heard and so have had a legal trial, whereby he might have appealed'. One MP was sure that the executions were 'done on purpose to put an affront upon the treaty [with the King] and to grieve and exasperate his Majesty'. Another 'resolute gentleman' stood up and addressed the speaker:

> I know, not withstanding what is otherwise pretended in this letter, that neither the town of Colchester, nor the county of Essex, desired any severity to be used towards those gentlemen and therefore I suppose this pretence of justice was wholly an act of revenge, and I fear out of a more private consideration than a public.

The MP was referring to what was widely believed to be a vendetta between Fairfax and Lucas which went all the way back to the battle of Marston Moor in 1643. Lucas had been captured by Fairfax, but given his freedom after pledging his word never to take up arms against Parliament again. Evidence of this bitter rift surfaced again during the siege itself, when Fairfax refused to have any contact at all with Sir Charles, concluding that he 'was not capable of command or trust in military affairs' because he had violated his parole. That slur provoked a long letter of rebuttal from Lucas, sent through the lines to the General, on 19 June. 'Concerning me, as being a prisoner still unto your Lordship', Lucas wrote: 'I purchased my freedom at a high rate, by a great sum of money'. This fine, or composition as it was known, for Royalist activities was paid into Goldsmith's Hall, London. For this, he insisted, 'according to the ordinances of the two Houses, I shall enjoy my freedom and estate'. But he claimed that 'when I was in peaceable manner in London', it was the Derby House Committee, set up to conduct the war on behalf of Parliament, which broke the terms of his parole, by putting a price on his head. Sir Charles said that he had no option but 'to retire myself to my own country and to my native town, for refuge, where my Lord, I do remain, not your prisoner, but your Lordship's humble servant'.

After the war even Fairfax's old chaplain, the Revd Spragg, waded into the controversy over Fairfax's motives. Lucas he said had given Fairfax 'so fatal a blow' at the battle of Marston Moor, that 'he [Fairfax] could never forgive him and for which stroke, in revenge it is thought, he took away his life at Colchester, having been often heard to threaten him'. Considering the enormous reputation that Fairfax had earned for chivalry among all sides in the Civil War, revenge as a motive does seem to be completely out of character. But the executions, coming after a distinguished and gallant military career, were to remain the only stain on Fairfax's otherwise unblemished humanitarian record.

Lucas and Lisle were instantly turned into martyrs in the Royalist cause. The loyal King's men, it was said, went to their deaths 'bravely', 'cheerfully', in true 'Roman' style, 'dreadless of death', They were 'scarce allowed time for their prayers'; they were 'massacred for their loyalty to their King, and love to their country'; they displayed 'magnanimity and true gallantry' in the 'doom of sudden death'. The 'liberty of the pulpit' was denied to protestors who wanted to eulogise them; they found an outlet for their prose, and even their poetry, in pamphlets. They warned in rhyme of the retribution that was brewing for the executioners: 'For who reflecting on this worthies fate/Vows not revenge 'gainst Fairfax and the State'.

Just over a month later Colonel Rainsborough, named by Carter as one of the 'spectators' at the execution of Lucas and Lisle, had his throat cut by three assassins at his temporary headquarters in Doncaster. He had been sent there to take over and 'tighten up the siege of Pontefract'. He probably died in a bungled kidnap attempt, but some pamphleteers were convinced that he was murdered 'for the death of Sir Charles Lucas and Sir George Lisle'. Nor would they [the Royalists] be satisfied merely 'with this new manner of murdering one that was faithful to Parliament ... but have further designs to take away the lives of at least fourscore other eminent men'. The hit-list was supposed to have included the names of Fairfax and Cromwell as well as Colonel Hammond, the Governor of the Isle of Wight where the King was being held prisoner, Colonel Pride, soon to become famous for purging Parliament of its Royalist-inclined MPs, and Major-General Lambert, one of the engineers of the recent Scots defeat. Among the aristocracy, Lord Saye and Sele and Lord Wharton, were also named. At the end of September a pamphlet entitled *A Dangerous and Bloudy Plot Discovered* revealed that

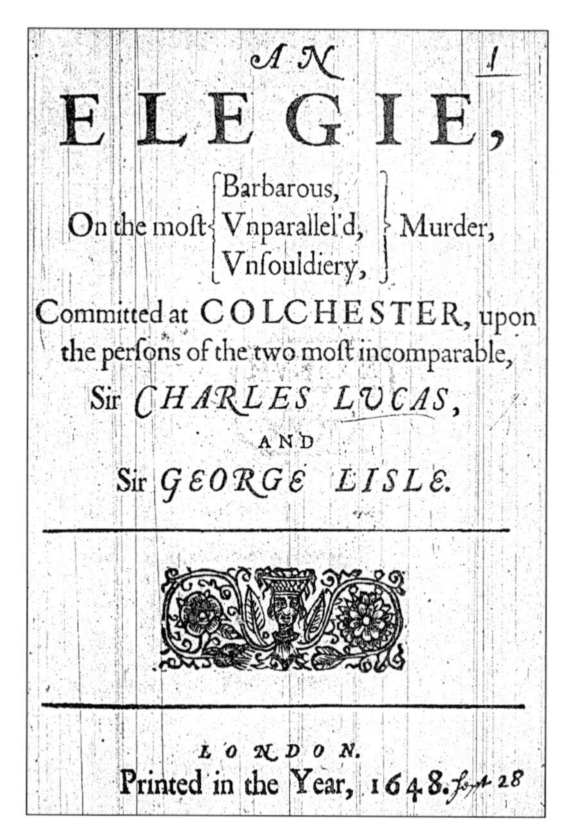

AN

ELEGIE,

On the moſt Barbarous, Vnparallel'd, Vnſouldiery, Murder,

Committed at COLCHESTER, upon the perſons of the two moſt incomparable,

Sir *CHARLES LUCAS*,

AND

Sir *GEORGE LISLE*.

LONDON.

Printed in the Year, 1648.

53. Lucas and Lisle soon became major figures in the Royalist Pantheon. Their eulogies were an indication of how bitter had become the dispute between the King and his radical opponents. By the end of the year the country had lurched into revolution and a month after that the King himself had been tried for treason and sent to the scaffold. (Essex County Council)

according to information given to the Derby House Committee and to the Speaker of the Commons 'there were divers of the King's party who had combined to massacre fourscore of the members of the Honourable House of Commons who, as they said, opposed the Treaty in the House'. It added: 'the destroyers cry peace, peace, but seek after blood'.

The Prince of Wales himself, in a personal letter to Fairfax, had already warned the General that reprisals could follow any mistreatment of Royalist prisoners. The letter, printed only five days before the surrender of Colchester, followed the collapse of the rebellion in South Wales and the capture of its leaders who, the Prince was at pains to point out, were prisoners of war 'under the authority of my commission'. He went on: 'I cannot but be extremely sensible of my own honour, which I take to be highly concerned in their preservation'. If they were harmed, he warned, 'a necessity will be put upon me of proceeding with such as fall into my hands in a way very contrary to my nature'. He added: 'I desire therefore that by your care and reasonable interposition, such moderation may be used toward them, as soldiers one to another'. The Prince no doubt considered that Fairfax was a moderate man and open to such reason, so he could not have been very satisfied with the cold reply he got back:

> I have acquainted the Houses with your Highness' Letter it being not in my power to act further, the Parliament having ordered in what way they [the Welsh leaders] shall be proceeded against, not so much that they were in hostility against them (I suppose) as that they have betrayed the trust reposed in them to the sad engaging in the second war and bloody.

Carter's own account of the siege of Colchester, first published in 1650 and quoted here at great length, was an undisguised tribute to his old commander, Sir Charles Lucas. In the preface, he called the executions 'a desire of revenge and thirst after blood'; the officers had sacrificed 'their blood for the honour of their sovereign and endeavouring to ease their oppressed country of an insupportable tyrannic burden'. Sir Charles, said Carter, 'was ever ready to afford what himself could not receive, free quarter; no not so much as one day's reprieve to prepare himself for his last voyage'. And he asked:

> who can justly accuse him, in the whole course of his actions or commands, with having laid his impetuous hand upon a submissive captive in cold blood, or ever suffered any blood to be split which he might, with honour or without prejudice to his command, spare.

The panegyric continued: 'never did a more undaunted spirit harbour more noble compassion, deeming nothing more inglorious than to domineer over the misery of a subdued enemy'. And so it went on.

The people seemingly forgotten in this spiral of vendetta were the rank and file of the Colchester garrison, but inevitably they too suffered in the violent aftermath of the war. The newsbooks and pamphlets mentioned them only in passing, while they covered in great depth the surrender negotiations and the fate of the gentlemen martyrs. Thus it was left to Carter to record in detail the harshness of their fate. Despite all of Fairfax's honeyed promises of amnesty – of allowing them to return home – few ever made it back to their own firesides. Instead they were treated with a brutality seldom before shown to English Protestant prisoners; the scale of the savagery meted out to fellow Englishmen was unknown in the First Civil War and unprecedented in the Second. It eloquently reflected the escalating cruelty of the civil strife. Carter explained:

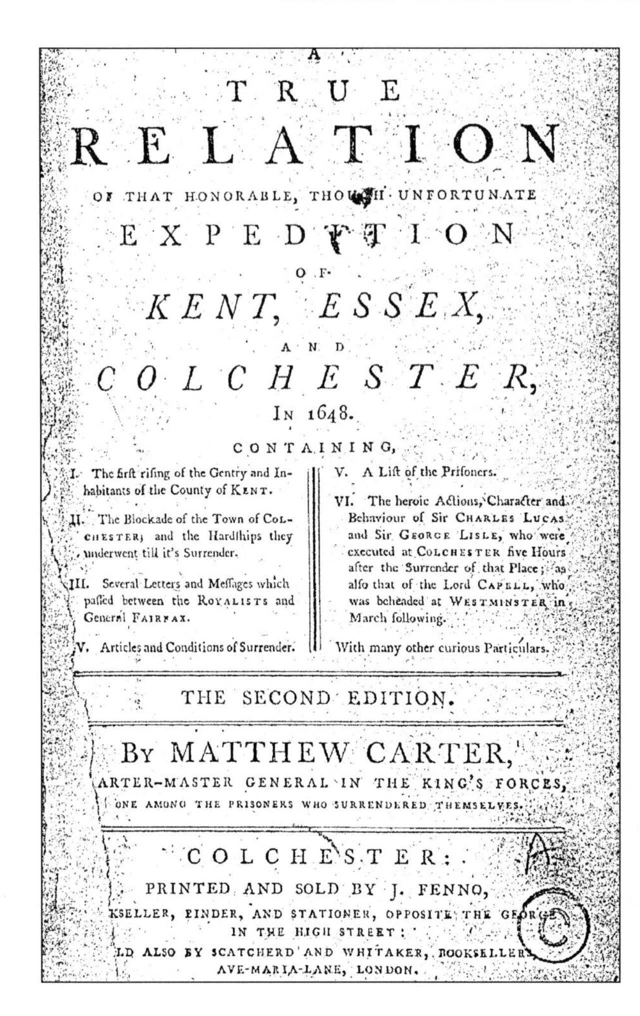

A

TRUE

RELATION

OF THAT HONORABLE, THOUGH UNFORTUNATE

EXPEDITION

OF

KENT, ESSEX,

AND

COLCHESTER,

IN 1648.

CONTAINING,

I. The first rising of the Gentry and Inhabitants of the County of KENT.

II. The Blockade of the Town of COLCHESTER; and the Hardships they underwent till it's Surrender.

III. Several Letters and Messages which passed between the ROYALISTS and General FAIRFAX.

V. Articles and Conditions of Surrender.

V. A List of the Prisoners.

VI. The heroic Actions, Character and Behaviour of Sir CHARLES LUCAS and Sir GEORGE LISLE, who were executed at COLCHESTER five Hours after the Surrender of that Place; as also that of the Lord CAPELL, who was beheaded at WESTMINSTER in March following.

With many other curious Particulars.

THE SECOND EDITION.

BY MATTHEW CARTER,

ARTER-MASTER GENERAL IN THE KING'S FORCES,

ONE AMONG THE PRISONERS WHO SURRENDERED THEMSELVES.

COLCHESTER:

PRINTED AND SOLD BY J. FENNO,

KSELLER, BINDER, AND STATIONER, OPPOSITE THE GEORGE

IN THE HIGH STREET;

LD ALSO BY SCATCHERD AND WHITAKER, BOOKSELLERS,

AVE-MARIA-LANE, LONDON.

54. Matthew Carter, Quartermaster General to the Royalist rebels, wrote this, the fullest account of the siege of Colchester, very soon after the event. The legacy of the siege continued long after the surrender: this second edition of his memoirs was printed 140 years later.
(Essex County Council)

> The General [Fairfax] distributed the officers, as slaves to the galleys, to ransom themselves, and most of them did afterwards purchase their liberties, by giving as much as they were able for the same, and returned home.

The 'private soldiers and inferior officers were drawn from the line and shut up in the churches'; their ordeal was just beginning.

The Parliamentary troops were given free reign to plunder anything they wanted from them and 'in a very short time there were very few or none left with any clothes on them and hardly shirts'. Thus beaten and stripped nearly naked, they began a death march across the length and breadth of the country. 'They marched them away', said Carter,

> on a day when it rained violently and conducted them from place to place in the country, lodging them in churches and such places, till many of them were starved and divers, who could not march by reason of their faintness, they pistolled them in the highways. Some they sold (as before they did the Scots) to be transported into foreign countries, from their wives and children, no matter to what part of the world.

Many ended up as virtual slaves on the plantations of Barbados: 'Prodigious numbers were also conveyed to several prisons, as far distant from their homes as they could contrive, some to Windsor, others to Oxford, Lynn in Norfolk, Warwick, Pendennis and St Michael's Mount in Cornwall'. Others were driven like cattle to Arundel, Gloucester, Hereford, and Cardiff.

Yet, at the end of the day, another round of the Civil War had once more failed to settle anything – only now the violence had grown in scale further polarising the factions. The King still survived, his support among large sections of the political nation appeared stronger than ever, despite being beaten on the battlefield for a second time. The 'Saints' of the army presented to many the infinitely more frightening spectre of militant fanaticism and social upheaval. The soldiers, many still unpaid, complained that all their sacrifice seemed to have changed nothing and they sensed a sell-out to the King by the waverers at Westminster. The radicals of the once more victorious New Model Army were winding themselves up for further, even more desperate measures. The surrender of Colchester and apparent victory for the godly cause, left only an ominous air of prescient revolution hanging in its wake. What would happen now was anyone's guess.

COUP D'ÉTAT

In his isolation at Carisbrooke Castle on the Isle of Wight the King still tried to behave like an unbeaten monarch and the Presbyterian-dominated Parliament, despite everything, continued to negotiate a treaty which would bring him back to his throne. But he was a weary and rapidly ageing man. His cheeks had sunk, deep pouches had appeared under his eyes and his hair and beard had turned grey. He was treated with courtesy, but allowed only a handful of retainers to wait upon him. He played occasional games of bowls, but was banned from hunting, his preferred pastime, in case it afforded him an opportunity to escape. He was allowed to keep only two dogs, his spaniel, Rogue and his favourite greyhound, Gypsy. He was a profoundly religious man and read the Bible a great deal and some poetry. He was also a devoted family man and found it deeply distressing that he had not seen his beloved wife Henrietta Maria for four years and his children for at least twelve months. He wavered between despair and flashes of optimistic fantasy. With an unflinching belief that he had been chosen by God himself to rule as king, he continued his Byzantine plots to retain his regal powers intact. Secret messages were smuggled in and out in laundry baskets and the fingers of gloves. He rightly suspected that there were spies everywhere watching him; there were endless rumours of attempts to assassinate him. He was under no illusion that his real enemies were not in Parliament, but in the radical ranks of the army: for them it was vital that he should be brought to book legally and publicly for his 'crimes' and not conveniently murdered in secret. They, like him, were morally convinced of their cause.

The King's popularity, after so many years of civil strife, was actually on the increase. Only a handful of people could even contemplate the possibility of bringing his near-sacred person to trial, let alone execution. The army-inclined *Moderate* newspaper could only wonder at this popular phenomenon and ridicule it:

> Doth not the kingdom know that his gracious majesty, who formerly endeavoured to introduce Popery and superstition into this nation, is now become a lover of the God's people and a promoter of the great work of reformation in the kingdom, in settling Presbyterian government and joining with the Presbyterian party against the Independent Army?

Pouring on the irony it continued: 'Doth not his extraordinary hatred of Cavaliers, who have hitherto engaged with him against the Parliament and the kingdom, give an ample demonstration of his late conversion?'

The King's continued popularity with large sections of the mainly conservatively minded populace was a huge irritation to radical groups like the Levellers. They deplored the inconsistency of the 'rude multitude, having no good or solid principles ... so that they are sometimes for the king and sometimes for Parliament and sometimes for both'. A popular ballad in London at the time ran:

> Then let's have King Charles, says George./Nay, we'll have his son, says Hugh,/Nay, then let's have none, says jabbering Jane,/ Nay, we'll all be kings, says Prue.

After six anarchic years without any settled form of government the country was desperate for stability. A regular foreign visitor, returning to England at about this time, could not believe the change that had come over the friendly and good humoured people he used to know; they had become 'melancholy and spiteful as if bewitched'. Taxation, still at wartime rates, was crippling, especially the excise, a purchase tax which pushed up the price of most essential goods. Supporters of the King were forced to 'compound', what amounted to a fine for supporting the Royalist cause. The amount was dependent on the extent of their participation in the war effort against Parliament and their ability to pay. Many small tradesmen, as well as large landowners, were brought to the brink of ruin by it. Some of the less scrupulous on the winning side were seen to be doing dishonestly well out of the victory, but the poorer sort were no better off. The army were forced to live at free quarter on the people they were supposed to be defending, because they hadn't been paid and limbless veterans joined the widows and orphans of those who had died in battle begging on the streets. Highway robbery increased, as did piracy in the coastal shipping lanes because of the lack of naval protection. Trade and industry were in tatters and, on top of everything, the country was having its third wet summer in a row causing widespread crop failure and near-starvation in many areas: never in the entire seventeenth century were grain prices to be higher. Most of the hard-pressed population may have considered it tantamount to sacrilege to lay hands on the King but, dazed as they were by this endless social disruption, they were no longer willing to leap, once again, to his defence. They were shocked by events, but prepared to accept them. They craved peace and a return to normality from the hands of anyone able to give it to them.

In this malaise the army was the only organisation left in the country with power enough to impose a settlement, but the army was becoming more unmanageable and politically motivated by the day. The men had remained unpaid for months by a Parliament who were still obviously intent on disbanding them without their arrears. Once more they felt that they had won the war, but were fast losing the peace. They were being betrayed by the politicians. Radicalism flourished in this atmosphere, helped on by civilian firebrands like the Levellers, who were intent on forcing through social change while the opportunity to do so still existed. As October progressed most regiments were in a dangerously volatile state. Agitators began to appear again in the ranks and pamphlets stoked up the political temperature. Some of Ireton's regiment refused direct orders from General Fairfax to disperse to their quarters. They passed a resolution saying: 'The King hath betrayed the trust reposed in him and raised war against this nation to enslave it; he is guilty of all the blood in these intestine wars'.

It was becoming increasingly clear that Fairfax was losing control of his troops. A courageous genius on the battlefield, he was no man for the cut and thrust of the political skirmishes now developing. The real leadership was being usurped by Henry Ireton, Oliver Cromwell's son-in-law. He doubtless acted with the counsel and approval of the Civil War's greatest leader, even though Cromwell was still far away from the political action in the north, trying to reduce the Royalist stronghold of Pontefract Castle. Ireton was prepared to ride the tiger of revolt, while moderates like Fairfax, were being left floundering in the turbulence. At one point Ireton, so frustrated by Fairfax's conservative inaction and determination to keep the army neutral and apolitical, tendered his resignation. It was 'not agreed to' and anyway was probably more of a gesture, because his initial despair soon turned to a stern resolution. He would finish the job himself and bring this criminal King to trial, by whatever means possible. At the beginning of October he made his agenda plain: it was 'high time [to] clear the House [of Commons] again with a new purge of impeachment'. He threw his weight behind a radical campaign of regimental petitions to Fairfax.

The Lord General, his title was handed down to him on the death of his father in March 1648, received more than twenty such petitions before the end of the year, twelve giving specific support to the Leveller programme. He could not contain the tide, but he refused to resign, only too aware of the dangers that lay in wait should army discipline fall apart altogether. A third civil war was to him a dreadfully real spectre: indeed it was one which would haunt the entire country for many years to come. Cromwell, in the final year of his life ten years later, warned: 'if we run into another flood of blood and war this nation ... must sink and perish utterly'. Duty kept Fairfax in his place, doubtless hoping that the calls for the King' s trial and ultimate execution were nothing more than noisy threats made to frighten the monarch into submission; like many other people he could not believe that they would actually end in his death. Regicide, for old soldiers of traditional breeding like Fairfax, was unthinkable, right up until the eleventh hour. He concentrated all his energies on the welfare of his men: and in reality getting them their just deserts after six years of war would probably have been the best way to defuse the time-bomb of revolution, if indeed there was enough time left to do that.

Events, from the beginning of November, began to accelerate at an alarming rate. By 15 November the army council had been taken over by belligerent radicals. They issued a statement calling for the capital punishment of the King, proposing a new constitution for the country based on the Levellers' *Agreement of the People* manifesto. Their move was given added urgency by a resolution passed on the same day by the peace party in the Commons calling for 'the King to be settled in a condition of honour, freedom and safety, agreeable to the laws of the land'. Parliament and army were diverging at a incredible speed. The time had come for army action, before these same MPs had a chance to outflank it by bringing the King back to his capital amid mounting popular acclaim.

The army moved its headquarters nearer to London – from St Albans to Windsor – and on 28 November the officers decided to occupy the city itself, despite a brave resolution in the Commons for the removal of Fairfax from his command, even though events now had little at all to do with him. On 30 November the army mustered in Hyde Park and the next morning marched into the city. It demanded, and got, £40,000 from the city's institutions towards their pay arrears, which still stood at £120,000. The same day, in driving sleet at five o'clock in the morning, the King, surrounded by radical officers and a troop of cavalry, was moved from the Isle Wight to the grim mainland fortress of Hurst Castle, which stood isolated on a spit of shingle on the Solent just south of Lymington. He thought it was a prelude to his assassination, but in fact from here he could be transferred to London, under close guard, at a moment's notice, with less risk of escape.

By 2 December army headquarters had been set up in Whitehall, although Fairfax now kept to his own house in Queen Street and attended few of the meetings of the army council. He had been comprehensively sidelined. The streets around Charing Cross were packed with soldiers and many of the resident gentry, sensing the trouble to come, abandoned their town houses for the safety of the country. The moderates in Parliament remained determined to push on with their negotiations with the King for 'the settlement of the peace of the Kingdom'. Ireton called together a committee of three radical MPs and three officers to discuss what to do about this. He was in favour of the immediate dissolution of Parliament, but the MPs successfully argued instead for a purge of all the pro-treaty members, a less drastic move for which there was a precedent and which, they hoped, would preserve some semblance of legality.

It was only then that Ireton went to see Fairfax to tell him of the decision. The General said later:

> I had not the least intimation of it 'til it was done ... Why it was so secretly carried out, that I should get no notice of it, was because I always prevented those designs when I knew them. But [by] this purging of the House the Parliament was brought into such a consumptive and languishing condition, as it could never again recover [a] healthful constitution.

What became known to history as Pride's Purge, the completion of the army's *coup d'état,* took place on the morning of 6 December.

The MPs who showed up for business were greeted with civility at the top of the steps into the lobby of the House by Colonel Pride, a former brewer's drayman, with a list of names in his hand. The building had been surrounded by armed troops. All the MPs who had voted for a treaty with the King together with all those who had failed to condemn the Scots invasion of the country in July, were refused entry. Some were sent home, but forty-one of them were placed under arrest and spent an uncomfortable day and night nearby in a freezing cellar. The following night they were made more comfortable at various inns in Westminster and slowly, one by one, released over the next few weeks. The army said that they were protecting the other MPs from the oppressive 'depravations' of self-interested and corrupt factions. Oliver Cromwell arrived the following day, from the siege of Pontefract, protesting that he knew nothing of the Purge, although he approved of it now that it had happened. Although historians have tried to link him to its planning, it is highly likely that he was telling the truth. He would have been far happier with a more subtly legalistic method of dealing with the crisis.

The council of officers of the army now controlled Parliament. They were the effective government of the country. On 15 December they decided that it was time to move the captive King to Windsor 'in order to the bringing of him speedily to justice'. The scene was set for the ultimate act of revolution, the trial and the execution of Charles I.

7

THAT WHICH HE COULD NOT REPENT OF

Following Pride's Purge the army felt secure enough to go after the King himself. He was described as this 'capital and grand offender', the 'author of all our troubles', the man 'guilty of all the loss, hazard and expense of the blood and mischiefs that have happened in the late wars of this kingdom'.

Oliver Cromwell had finally arrived in the capital the day after the Purge, bringing down on his head the odium of all conspiracy theorists. It was alleged then, and still is, that he was himself the Machiavellian author of events who had cynically dallied in the north waiting only to make a dramatic entrance after the dirty work had been done for him by his acolytes. In fact he had been ordered by a desperate Fairfax to return to headquarters from Pontefract, where he was mopping up the last remnants of armed Royalist resistance. Fairfax no doubt hoped that Cromwell's great influence with the men and his experience as an MP would help bring stability to 'the very great business now in agitation', even though he knew that his second-in-command sympathised with much of the radicals' religious ideology. As early as 20 November Cromwell had told Fairfax that he sympathised with his men when they demanded 'to have justice done upon the offenders' adding 'from my heart [I] concur with them'. There were very good military reasons for him to remain in the north while he 'settled the counties' and the appalling weather of that autumn had made speedy travel impossible, turning roads into quagmires and rivers into often uncrossable torrents. He had every good reason to be late.

It seems probable that Cromwell, even at this late stage, had still not made up his own mind about what should be done with this stubborn monarch who steadfastly refused to come to terms with reality, but at least he looked decisive when he finally arrived. He took up residence in the royal suite at Whitehall and sometimes held audience sprawled on one of the King's beds. Its still not clear when he made up his mind that the King had to die – probably when it became clear that the monarch had no intention of abdicating. He certainly struggled to preserve a legalistic front on all that was happening, even meeting the captive Duke of Hamilton two or three times in an effort to get an admission that the King had been behind the Scots invasion of July. The duke steadfastly refused to implicate Charles to the end, robbing the prosecutors of the hard evidence needed to prove conclusively that he had conspired to make war on his own people. The debate about the King's fate and the shape of the country's future constitution – whether or not it should become a republic – raged in both Parliament and the army. No-one of any stature in the country wanted to lead the attack on so sacrosanct an institution as the monarchy.

It was with huge difficulty that anyone was found to sit on a special High Court of Justice to try Charles. It was envisaged as a giant tribunal of over 100 men of substance drawn from a broad sweep of the political nation. But most refused to lend their name to such proceedings; none of the half a dozen peers sympathetic to Parliament would sit and neither would any of the country's existing high court judges. In the end only half the number of named commissioners were willing to show their faces. Fairfax, whose presence would have lent urgently needed credibility to the proceedings, had attended only the first preliminary meeting on 8 January, had refused even to sit down and had never again attended. When the court assembled and his name was called as a judge a woman in a mask had shouted out: 'He has more wit than to be here'. It was the spirited Lady Anne Fairfax, who was obviously acting without the knowledge of her husband. She was silenced only when some of the guards, there in strength under the command of Lieutenant-Colonel Daniel Axtell, pointed their muskets at her with orders to fire if there was any more commotion.

The King appeared closely flanked by soldiers and when the charges against him were read out – that he was a 'tyrant, traitor and murderer and a

55. Lady Anne Fairfax, Thomas Fairfax's spirited wife: unknown to her husband (he became third Baron Fairfax after the death of his father in March 1648) she repeatedly interrupted the trial of the King by shouting protests from behind a mask in the public gallery. The guard threatened to shoot her after she yelled that Oliver Cromwell was a traitor.

public and implacable enemy of the Commonwealth of England' – he wanted to know by what authority he had been summoned before them: 'I do stand more for the liberty of my people than any here that come to be my pretended judges', he said. The King's sudden eloquence – his usually embarrassing stutter had completely disappeared – took the court president, John Bradshaw, by surprise. Wearing a steel-lined hat as a precaution against assassins, he ordered that the royal prisoner should be removed by Axtell's guards, who noisily called for 'Justice! Justice!' as they hustled him out, causing him maximum discomfort by trying to blow handfulls of gunpowder into his eyes. Some of the assembled crowd of spectators yelled 'God save the King'. The same circular argument continued for another three days as the King persisted in challenging the legality of the court. Finally, after considering some flimsy evidence in closed session, his judges predictably decided to sentence him to death. It had been a chaotic travesty of a show trial.

As Bradshaw began the sentence with the words: 'in the name of the people of England', Lady Fairfax, again from the public gallery and from

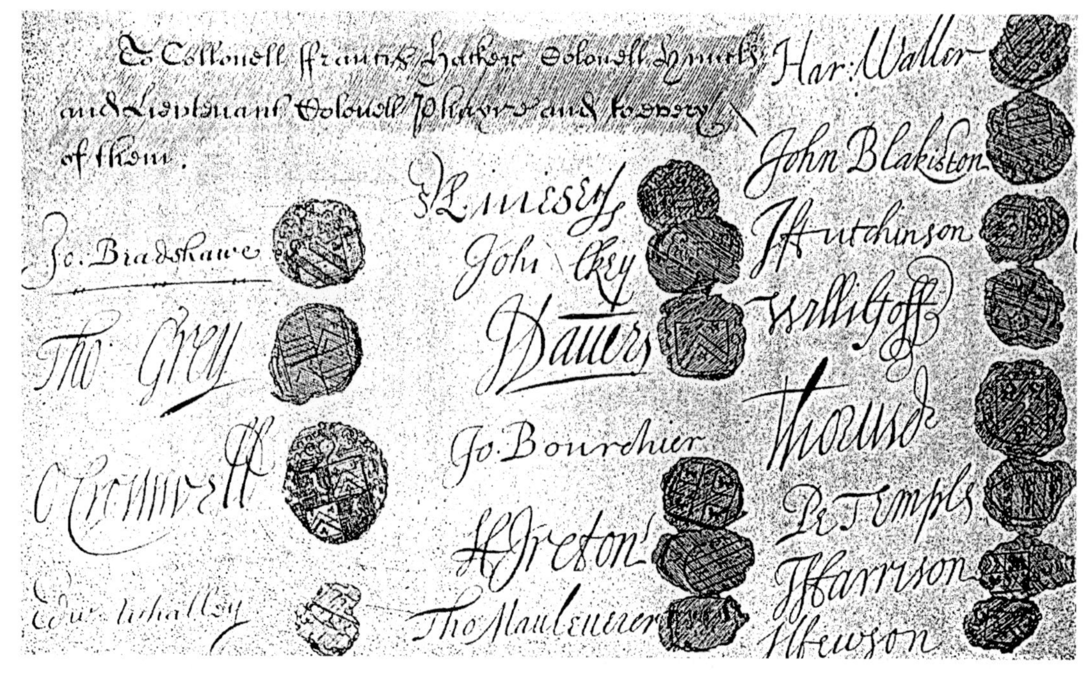

To Collonell ffrancis Hacker, Colonell Huncks and Lieutenant Colonell Phayre and to every of them.

Jo. Bradshawe
Tho: Grey
O Cromwell
Edw. Whalley
John Okey
J Danvers
Jo. Bourchier
H Ireton
Tho Mauleverer
Har: Waller
John Blakiston
J Hutchinson
Willi Goffe
Tho Pride
Pe Temple
T Harrison
J Hewson

56. Some of the first signatures on the death warrant of Charles I: John Bradshaw, the president of the tribunal, appears first, followed by Thomas Grey and then Oliver Cromwell.

behind a mask, risked the muskets of Axtell's guards to shout her protest: 'Not a half of them, not a quarter of the people of England. Oliver Cromwell is a traitor'. She was quickly pushed out of harm's way by friends. Through the ensuing uproar the King asked several times to be heard, but he was shouted down by Bradshaw. The guard contemptuously blew tobacco smoke into his face as they led him away. Fairfax made two attempts to have the sentence postponed, once on 29 January at the council of officers, and again on the following day, just hours before the axe fell. He did nothing more despite entreaties from Edward Stephens, one of the purged MPs, who told him: 'The power is now yours; rouse yourself my lord!' Fairfax seemed paralysed by inaction and indecision. One witness described him as 'much distressed in his mind and changed purposes often every day'.

Only fifty-nine of the King's judges could be found to put their names to the execution warrant and when Charles stepped out on to the scaffold he found a phalanx of mounted troopers between him and a crowd of onlookers. His final words to them went unheard, before the headsman decapitated him with one fatal blow. The hushed throng of civilians let out a low moan at the enormity of what had been done, before they were scattered by troops who swept in from Charing Cross. Within minutes the streets were empty.

On 6 February the House of Commons, – the 'Rump' of the original Long Parliament – abolished the House of Lords as 'useless and dangerous', and the following day the office of King. A third of the newly nominated council of state were military men, even though Henry Ireton, the arch-plotter, was rejected as a member – a bitter rebuff to his political ambitions.

A THORN REMOVED

The weeks following the King's execution were marked by a series of 'war crimes' trials. Among those sent to the scaffold were the Duke of Hamilton, who led the doomed Scottish invasion of July and August and the Earl of Holland who was taken by surprise at St Neots while on a hopeless attempt to relieve Colchester. Then on 7 March it was the turn of the aristocrats who organised the defence of Colchester: the Earl of Norwich was charged, under his former title of Lord Goring, at the same time as Lord Capel. While Capel, renowned as a dashing commander of Royalist infantry, disdained to plead for his life, the aged Lord Goring threw himself on the mercy of the court to 'give him leave to live'. According to Carter he tried to 'reconcile his judges to him': he spoke of 'being bred up in the court from his cradle at the time of Queen Elizabeth; of his having been a servant of King James all his reign [and] of his obligations to the crown and his endeavours to serve it'.

Capel was made of sterner stuff, the material from which heroes are made. Before his trial began he had succeeded in escaping from the Tower of London by slipping down a rope, wading through a ditch up to his chin in water, before being met by friends on the outside and taken to a safe house in the Temple. There he lay low for two or three nights, waiting for the hue and cry to die down, before trying to move to a safer refuge at Lambeth Marsh. On the way, however, his escort let slip his title in conversation, addressing him as 'My Lord'. A sharp-eared boatman followed them to the hideout and turned him in for the reward of £10.

At his trial Lord Capel 'appeared undaunted and utterly refused to submit to their jurisdiction'. He was a soldier and a prisoner of war: 'the lawyers and gown-men had nothing to do with him and therefore he would not answer anything which they had said against him'. He insisted that the 'law of nations' exempted prisoners from death 'if it was not inflicted' in the heat of battle or within so many days of it, 'which were long since expired'. He claimed that he had been told by Fairfax himself, after the execution of

Lucas and Lisle, that 'no other lives should be in danger'. Ireton, one of the judges in court, who of course had been at Colchester, denied that the General had made any such promise, and even if he had 'Parliament's authority could not be restrained thereby'. He also put the aristocrat 'in mind of his carriage at the time and how much he neglected the General's civility'. Clearly Carter saw malice behind Ireton's every move. Capel then asked that Fairfax should be brought to court to give evidence on the matter. The Lord General did not appear, but the question was sent to him and evidence given that he had denied such a 'direct and positive promise'. At most he could only 'exempt those prisoners from being tried before a court, or a council of war [which] could not be understood as an obligation upon Parliament'. It was Parliament which had to decide on how 'the peace and safety of the kingdom' was to be maintained, he said.

The sentence of death on Lord Capel seemed an inevitable formality, even though he demanded his right, under 'the law of the land', to be tried by a court of his noble peers. His fate was pronounced by John Bradshaw, the same man who had sentenced the King little more than a month before. Capel, he said sarcastically, had been 'tried by the judges that Parliament thought fit to assign him and ... Who had judged a better man than himself [the King]'.

The Earl of Norwich escaped execution by a hair's breadth. He had 'always lived a cheerful and jovial life', Carter recalled, 'without contracting many enemies, had many there who wished him well and few who had animosity against him'. The result was that the tribunal divided equally for and against him 'so that his life depended on the single [casting] vote of the speaker [of the House of Commons]'. Carter thought that the Speaker William Lenthall felt obligated to 'save a man's life who was put to ask [for] it in that place' and 'by this fortune he came to be preserved'. Not so Capel. All the appeals made by his friends and family to save his life failed – including bribes of cash 'to some, who were willing to receive it and made promises accordingly'. A petition to commute the death sentence went to the House of Commons and 'many gentlemen spoke in his behalf'. Capel had never made any bones about where his allegiances lay; he could in no manner be condemned, like many others, of duplicity against Parliament; he had always 'resolutely declared himself for the King' and this honourable stance was pleaded on his behalf. Even Oliver Cromwell 'who had known him well', said Carter, 'spoke so much good of him that all men thought he was now safe'. But Cromwell ultimately came down in favour of his execution: Capel, he concluded,

57. The dashing Royalist leader Lord Capel: he was put on trial for his part in the siege of Colchester, but only after first managing a daring escape from the Tower of London. He was recaptured after several days of liberty and then refused to recognise the court which ordered his execution. Cromwell thought him too dangerous an opponent to be allowed to live. (Colchester Museums)

58. William Lenthall, Speaker of the House of Commons during the turbulent years of the Civil War: it was his casting vote which saved the aged Earl of Norwich, the Royalists' nominal commander at Colchester, from the block. The High Court of Justice failed to agree on whether or not Norwich should be executed.

> would be the last man in England who would forsake the royal interest. He had great courage, industry and generosity, he had many friends who would always adhere to him and that as long as he lived, what condition so ever he was in, he would be a thorn in their sides, and therefore for the good of the Commonwealth, he should give his vote against the petition.

Ireton, of course, could be counted on to speak against Capel 'as a man he was heartily afraid of'.

Capel, a devoted family man, sent two tender letters of farewell to his 'disconsolate lady'. He wrote: 'I beseech thee take care of thy health; sorrow not unsoberly, unusually. God be unto thee better than an husband and to my children better than a father. I am sure He is able to be so'. He walked to the scaffold in Westminster 'saluting such of his friends and acquaintances who he saw there, with a serene countenance'. Before bowing his head to the block he told those gathered near that he was about to die 'for doing that which he could not repent of.'

A BATTERED TOWN

Colchester, or rather the wreck of the town that was left, was never the same again. Ten years later John Evelyn remarked that it remained 'wretchedly demolished by the siege'. It never regained its pre-war position as one of the country's leading industrial and commercial centres. More than seventy-five years later its battle scars were still plain for all to see. In the 1720s the prominent writer and journalist Daniel Defoe paid it a visit. It was populous and boasted some fine, well-built houses, he said, and 'streets fair and beautiful'. But he added: 'It still mourns, in the ruins of the Civil War the battered walls, the breaches in the turrets and the ruined churches still remain'. The parish church of St Mary's at the Walls had been rebuilt, although its tower remained a stump, still shattered by Parliamentary shelling. Meanwhile: 'The lines with the forts built by the besiegers and which surrounded the whole town, remained very visible in many places, but the chief of them are demolished'.

Fairfax had levied a fine of £14,000 on the town for their 'delinquency' in admitting the Royalist army in the first place 'with which sum', Carter explained, 'he purposed to pay the Army'. It was a huge amount to find for a community already devastated by the fighting and it was hardly surprising that it 'fell short of what was demanded'. Carter attempted to list the sums that were paid over in the North and Head Wards of the town 'but those paid in the East and South Wards could not be learned'. The wealthy Head Ward contributed £3,300, with two prominent citizens, Messrs Buckstone and Thurston handing over £500 each. In North Ward only £643 was gathered in smaller amounts – one contribution amounted only to eight pounds. This was hardly going to be enough to satisfy the victors, even when Colchester's substantial community of Dutch textile workers were asked to find much more than their fair share, so the fine was spread outwards to include 'malignant' Royalists in the rest of the county who were suspected of giving their backing to the rising.

Under the direction of the army, the town council was purged of all but its most radical Puritan members, but for the rest of the Interregnum, before the restoration of monarchy twelve years later, they had to rely on military backing to keep them in power. Troops had to be stationed in

59. Evidence of the siege can still be seen in Colchester, more than 350 years later. St Botolphs Priory stood just outside the old town wall and was devastated in the fighting.

60. Just down the road from St Mary at the Walls, the remains of the old town wall leans over at a drunken angle: it was left that way by Fairfax who ordered the destruction of Colchester's fortifications.

Colchester to prevent the plundering of 'the Roundheads and the Independents'. Later, in the 1650s, there were reports of an attempt within the town to drum up support for another, but this time abortive, Royalist rising. Even after the death of Cromwell and restoration of the monarchy, the public life of Colchester continued to be defined by its religious and political faction. And, as if the town had not had its full share of catastrophe, more than 5,000 people perished in the plague of 1665, a greater number by far than anywhere else in Essex and even more, proportionally, than died in London.

The saga of the siege of Colchester was continually recycled. Very soon after Charles II was restored in 1660 visitors began asking to be shown the spot, under the castle walls, where Lucas and Lisle faced the firing squad. The grass, so local legend had it, refused to grow there: it was suggested early in the eighteenth century that this may have been achieved 'by art for the sake of getting money by showing people this lying wonder'.

After their execution the bodies of Lucas and Lisle were taken to St Giles Church, to be interred in the Lucas family vault. After the Restoration,

Lord John Lucas, Sir Charles's elder brother who had fled Colchester prior to the siege and spent the Second Civil War keeping a low profile in London, had a marble slab carved to cover their resting place. It can be read to this day, in St Giles Church. It records that these 'two most valiant captains ... for their eminent loyalty to their sovereign' were, on the 28 August 1648, 'by the command of Sir Thomas Fairfax (the General of the Parliament army) in cold blood barbarously murdered'. Fairfax's daughter, who by then was married to the Duke of Buckingham, objected to the slur on her father's good name and her husband applied to the sovereign to have the stone destroyed. Instead the new monarch ordered that the words should be carved even more deeply into the marble to ensure that the memory of the martyrs remained for posterity.

Sir Thomas Fairfax, the victor of Colchester and a Parliamentary hero of the Civil War, did not serve the Republic for long after the King's execution. Together with his loyal and spirited wife Anne, he quit the public arena, but not before he had helped Cromwell to deal with a fresh challenge to the authority of the army 'Grandees' from the radicals in their midst. With the execution of the King, a Leveller-inspired mutiny once more broke out in the ranks at Salisbury. The rebels made their way north to link up with other disaffected units, but were brought to bay at Burford Church in the Cotswolds. Three were shot as an example to the others, while a fourth ringleader, according to Leveller memory, bought his life by agreeing to renounce the cause and justify 'all those wicked and abominable proceedings of the General (Cromwell) [by] howling and weeping like a crocodile' from the pulpit. It was the last such rebellion that Cromwell had to face from his rank and file and it marked the end of the radical phase of the English Revolution.

Cromwell was a religious radical, but was no social revolutionary. He believed in strict conservative stratification, a pecking order of noblemen, gentlemen and yeomen. But his attempts to reconcile his new regime to members of the old ruling establishment repeatedly failed, robbing it of the legitimacy and stability it so badly needed. The Republic and the Commonwealth, which he created in the Interregnum years in which he became Lord Protector, had to be sustained always by a promptly paid and highly disciplined military machine, purged of its extremists and willing to do as it was told. The government remained a minority one, backed by swordsmen: the views of the soldiery could never be ignored, even by the Lord Protector Cromwell himself, a king in all but name. Their objections weighed a great deal with him when, as Lord Protector in 1657, he rejected

61. The spot where Lucas and Lisle were shot by firing squad, behind the castle, quickly became a shrine for visiting Royalist pilgrims, as well as for the merely curious tourist, after the Restoration of the monarchy in 1660. The execution is still commemorated there today with this stone.

62. A tombstone for the two Royalist martyrs, Lucas and Lisle, still survives in St Giles Church, which housed the crypt of the Lucas family. It records that they were 'in cold blood barbarously murdered' at the command of Sir Thomas Fairfax. After the Restoration Fairfax's daughter objected to this slur on the family name, but the new king, Charles II, disagreed. He ordered that the epitaph should be etched even more deeply into the marble.

repeated offers of the crown itself. He would never, he declared, rebuild Jericho, and 'set up that that providence hath destroyed and laid in the dust'.

His first priority, after Charles's execution in 1649, was to consolidate his version of the revolution, by first dealing with radical challenges to his authority at home and controversially subduing Ireland and then Scotland. The invasion of Scotland was more than Fairfax could tolerate and at last on 25 June, 1650 he finally resigned his commission. Cromwell's failure to carry with him such a thoroughly respected pillar of the orthodox gentry was a great blow in his later efforts to evolve a political system that would 'heal and settle' the deep scars inflicted on British society by the Civil War.

Fairfax, respected for his courage, chivalry and inspired leadership in battle, retired to his Yorkshire estates to breed horses, write poetry and enrich his

63. Oliver Cromwell, as he was viewed at the year of his death in 1658. The three British crowns of England, Scotland and Ireland, are impaled on his sword, while in his left hand he carries a Bible. Although Cromwell was repeatedly offered the crown he turned it down, saying he would never rebuild the walls of Jericho.

64. Sir Thomas Fairfax became Lord Fairfax, after the death of his father in 1648: he resigned his commission rather than lead the New Model Army on its pacification of Scotland in 1650. A political moderate, he tried ineffectually to save the King from execution and spent the Interregnum quietly on his Yorkshire estates. He eventually joined the delegation which was sent to Holland in 1660 to invite the young Charles II back to his throne.

65. *Eikon Basilike* – the image of Charles I as a martyr: the King achieved almost saintly status among some sections of Royalist opinion. Here he is pictured reviewing the principal events of his reign. The book, *Eikon Basilike* (Royal Image) was sold illegally and reprinted thirty times in the year following his death. Paradoxically the King had seldom been as popular as he was at the time of his execution.

library. He remained at heart a constitutional monarchist, and when the Protectorate began to fall apart with the death of Cromwell in 1658 he raised his friends and neighbours in the north to support the march from Scotland of General Monck. As commander of the only well-disciplined and dependable military force left in the country Monck restored order. Fairfax declared for the election of a free and constitutional Parliament and agreed to be one of the commissioners who went to Holland to invite the young King Charles II to reclaim his throne. He was, however, characteristically appalled when Cromwell's rotting body was dug up and hung on a gibbet. But he also, according to his cousin, 'utterly abhorred and lamented the death of the King to his dying day and never mentioned it, but with tears in his eyes'.

Defeated Royalist retainers like Matthew Carter, the Quartermaster General of the Colchester garrison, watched horrified as their world turned violently upside down. For him 1648 was recognisably the last year of an old and already extinct way of life. It was, he wrote,

> a year of reproach and infamy above all years which had passed before it, a year of the highest dissimulation and hypocrisy, of the deepest villainy and most bloody treasons that any nation was ever cursed with: a year [of] atheism, infidelity and rebellion.

A mutated monarchy eventually managed to survive after the wreck of revolution: but its absolutism was tamed and Carter's reverential attitudes to it were gone forever.

REFERENCES

Full titles and details of books referred to can be found in the bibliography.

FOREWORD: A HUNT FOR THE BLOOD OF ALL THE NOBILITY

Carter, *True Relation*, pp.113.
Firth, *Clarke Papers*, pp.31–9.
Thomason Tracts: Parliament Porter, (September 11, 1648) & *Mercurius Pragmaticus*, (September 5, 1648).
Wood, *Riot, Rebellion and Popular Politics*, chapter 4, p.127.

1: I WONDER WE WERE SO MUCH DECEIVED

Abbott, *Speeches and Writings of Oliver Cromwell Vol. I*, pp.256, 364–5, 374–8, and 445–6.
Carlton, *Going to the Wars*, chapter 9.
Carter, *True Relation*, pp.113, 185–7.
Coward, *Oliver Cromwell*, chapter 2, p.28.
Coward, *Stuart Age*, chapter 6.
Davis, *Oliver Cromwell*, chapter 5.
Gardiner, *Great Civil War*, chaps XLI to XLV.
Gentles, *New Model Army*, chapter 7.
Hibbert, *Cavaliers and Roundheads*, pp.252–3.
Jones, *Royal Prisoner*, chapter 1.
Kishlansky, *Monarchy Transformed*, chapter 7.
Lilburn, *Impeachment of High Treason against Oliver Cromwell*, (London, 1649).
Morrill, Mutiny and Discontent in English Provincial Armies.
Morrill (ed.) *Scottish National Covenant*, chaps 5 and 6.
Roots, *Speeches of Oliver Cromwell*, p.30.
Roy, 'England Turned Germany'.
Shakespeare, *Troilus and Cressida*, Act I, Scene III.

2: LIKE A SNOWBALL INCREASING

Ashton, *Counter Revolution*, pp.106, 142–144, 145–147, 197, 215–223, 369–72, 375, 378, 415, 416–417, 464–467, and 473.
'From Cavalier to Roundhead Tyranny', pp.194–195.

Bell, *Memorials of the Civil War*, pp.32–34, and 36–38.
Byford, *Birth of Protestant Town*, pp.23–35.
Carter, *A True Relation*, pp.86–97, 105–106, and 108–115.
Clarendon, *History of the Rebellion*, *Vol. 4*, pp.287–288.
Diary or Account of the Siege, p.281–283.
Firth, *Clarke Papers*, pp.26–29.
Gentles, *New Model Army*, pp.243–246.
Hunt, *The Puritan Moment* pp.176, 272, and 295.
Manning, *English People and English Revolution*, pp.171–178.
Manning, *1649*, pp.84–87.
Thomason Tracts: The *Remonstrance and Declaration of the Knights*, 6 July, 1648, E451(11); The *Parliament Kite*, 29 June, 1648, E450(15); *Colchester Teares*, 31 July, 1648, E445(16); *Mercurius Britannicus*, 1 August, 1648, E445(12); *Declaration of Sir William Batten*, 21 August, E460(13).
Walter, *Colchester Plunderers*, chaps 2, 3 and Conclusion.
Wilson, *Fairfax: a Life*, p.131–132, 134–136.
Wood, *Riot, Rebellion and Popular Politics*, p.125.
1. Fairfax third Baron Fairfax after the death of his father in March.

3: SINNING AGAINST SO MUCH LIGHT

Ashton, *Counter Revolution*, pp.326, 332, 334–335, 367, 406, 409, 418–422, and 433–404.
Carter, *True Relation*, pp.115–123, 126–129, 133–134.
Firth, *Clarke Papers*. pp.28–29.
Coward, 'Why Charles I was executed', p.36.
Diary or Account of Siege, pp.284–286.
Kenyon, *The Civil Wars*, pp.63–64.
Morrill, *Scottish National Covenant*, pp.114, 125, 126, and 141.
Thomason Tracts: Mercurius Elencticus, 5 July, 1648, E451(9); *Mercurius Fidelicus*, 24 August, 1648, E460(32); *Mercurius Bellicus*, 27 June, 1648, E449(44); The *Moderate*, 13 July, 1648, E452(27); The *Moderate*, 27 June, 1648, E450(8), *Colchester Teares;* 31 July, 1648, E445(16); *A True and exact relation of the taking of Colchester*, 31 August, 1648, E461(24); *Mercurius Psitacus*, 24 July, 1648, E453(44), *Mercurius Pragmaticus*, 8 August, 1648, E457(12); *A Perfect Weekly Account*, 25 July, 1648, E454(3); *Parliament Vulture*, 22 June, 1648, E449(10);
Woolrych, *Battles*, pp.152-154 and 159–160.
2. A sucking fish which it was said attached itself to the bottom of ships so slowing down their progress through the water.

4: THOSE MERCILESSE MECHANICKS

Brenner, 'Civil War Politics and London'.
Carter, *True Relation*, pp.128, 133–137, 139, 143–147, 150–152, 167, 171.
Diary or Account of Siege, pp.286–287.
Donagan, 'Atrocity, War Crimes and Treason'.
Firth, *Clarke Papers*, pp.29–30.

Firth, *Memoirs of Edmund Ludlow*, pp.203–204.
Gentles, *New Model Army*, pp.239–241.
Hunt, *Puritan Moment*, p.284.
Kenyon, *Stuart Constitution*, pp.318–319.
Manning, *1649*, pp.239–241.
Manning, *Aristocrats, Plebeians and Revolution*, p.97.
Roberts, 'Agencies, Human and Divine', pp.10, 17 and 22–23.
Thomason Tracts, *Joyfull News from Colchester*, 17 July, 1648, E452(41); *From the Leaguer at Colchester*, 6 July, 1648, E451(28); The *Moderate Intelligencer*, 6 July, E451(15); 13 July, E452(28); 20 July, E453(29); 10 August, 1648, EA57(33); The *Moderate*, 29 June, E450(8); 18 July, E453(19); 25 July, E454(2); 22 August, 1648. E460(18); *Demands and Proposals of the Earle of Norwich*, 22 August, 1648, E460(25); *Mercurius Bellicus*, 27 June, E449(44); *Mercurius Britannicus*, 25 July, E454(7); *Mercurius Elencticus*, 5 July, E451(3), 2 August, E456(19); *Mercurius Melancholicus*, 17 June, E448(8), 6 July, E451(18) and 8 July, E451(29); 24 July, E453(43), 31 July, FA55(14); *Mercurius Pragmaticus*, 15 August, E458(25); *Mercurius Psitacus*, 26 June, E449(28), 17 July, E452(43), 3 July, E450(25), 24 July, E453(44); A *Wonder*, 6 July, E451(17); *Colchester Teares*; *Colchester Spie*, 11 August, E458(4); *A declaration of proceedings*, E451(8); *Parliamentary Kite*, 23 July, E452(24), 24 August, E460(31); *Perfect Weekly Account*, 28 June, E450(3), 19 July, E452(19); *Last Fight at Colchester*, 17 June, E448(6); *Diverse Remarkable Passages*, 20 July, E453(27); *Great Victory Obtained*, 23 June, E449(20); *Particulars of the Fight at Colchester*, 15 July, E448(11); *Discovery of the Intentions of the Army*, 11 July, 669fl2(75); *Resolution of the Army Concerning the City of London*, August 17, E459(18); *Declaration of His Highnesse the Prince of Wales*, 25 July, E454(8); *A declaration of proceedings*, E451(8).
Underdown, *Pride's Purge*, p.100.

5: THEY WILL NEVER FORGIVE YE

Ashton, *Counter Revolution*, pp.334–335, 367, 413–414, 437, 440–442, 464, 474.
'From Cavalier to Roundhead Tyranny'.
Bernard Capp, 'Naval Operations', in Kenyon (ed.), *The Civil Wars*, pp.108–184.
Carter, *True Relation*, pp.137–138, 148–149, 155–156, 159–172.
Diary or Account of Siege, p.287.
Firth, *Clarke Papers*, pp.30–31.
Thomason Tracts, A *great and bloudy fight at Colchester*, 1 July, E453(18); *The Prince of Wales Coming to Yarmouth*, 27 July, E454(18); *A Prospective Glasser or Revolters at Sea*, E460(39); *Prince Charles His Declaration Concerning the Citizens of London*, 28 July, E455(7); *A Declaration of Sir William Batten*, 21 August, E460(13); *Joyfull News from Colchester*, 17 July, E452(41); *Declaration of His Highnesse the Prince of Wales to Sir Marmaduke Langdale*, 25 July, E454(8); *Message from His Highnesse the Prince of Wales to the Major of Yarmouth*, E454(21); *Colchester Teares*; *A True and exact Relation of the taking of Colchester*, 31 August, E461(24); *Mercurius Britannicus*, 21 June, E449(5); June 27, E449(42); July 18, E453(10); July 25, E454(7); *A Letter Sent from aboard His Highnesse the Prince of Wales to the Royalists in Kent*, 25 August, E460(37); *Mercurius Bellicus*, 26 July, E454(11); The *Parliament Kite*, 20 July, E453(28); 3 August, E456(20); *Mercurius Britannicus*, 5 July, E 454(7); *Exact Narrative of Every dayes Proceedings since the Insurrection in Essex*, 18 June, E448(18); *A true and perfect Resolution of the Condition of the Noblemen*, 6 September, E462(16); *The Resolution of Sir Marmaduke Langdale*, 20 June, E448(21);

The *Kingdomes Weekly Intelligencer*, 29 August, E461(14).
Woolrych, *Battles of the English Civil War*, pp.158–177.

6: CONTRARY TO THE RULES OF HONOUR

Bell, *Memorials of the Civil War*, pp.44, 51, 52, 56–57.
Carter, *True Relation*, pp.v, vii–viii, 181–198, 200, 204–205.
Firth, *Clarke Papers*, pp.31–39.
Gentles, *New Model Army*, pp.266–289.
Roots, *Speeches of Oliver Cromwell*, p.185
Thomason Tracts, A *True and exact Relation of the taking of Colchester*, E461(24); A *True Relation of the Surrendering of Colchester*, 28 August, 669f13(7); *A Letter sent to the Honourable William Lental*, 28 August, E461(5); A *letter from his Excellency the Lord Fairfax*, 2 September, E461 (35); *Mercurius Pragmaticus*, 5 September, E462(8); *The Kingdome's Weekly Intelligencer*, 27 June, E449(45); The *Loyal Sacrifice*, 30 November, E 1202(2); The *Declaration and Remonstrance of the King's loyal subjects*, 4 September, E462(6); The *Perfect Weekly Account*, 23 August, E460(27); The *Parliament Porter*, 4 September, E462(3), 11 September, E462(26); The *Cruell Tragedy or Inhumane Butchery*, 2 September, E462(30); *Two Epitaphs*, 23 September, E464(32); *A full and exact relation of the Horrid murder*, 3 November, E470(4); *A Dangerous and Bloudy Plot Discovered*, 28 September, E465(21);
Wedgwood, *Trial of Charles I*, pp.14, 28–29, 30, 32–34, 41–46.
Wilson, *Fairfax*, 147.

7: THAT WHICH HE COULD NOT REPENT OF

Ashton, *Counter Revolution*, pp.408–409 and 478.
'From Cavalier to Roundhead Tyranny', pp.203–206.
James Burk, 'The New Model Army and the Problems of Siege Warfare', pp.1–28.
Carter, *True Relation*, pp.190–191 and 205–216.
Defoe, *A Tour*, pp.57–59.
Barbara Donagan, 'Atrocity War Crime and Treason', pp. 1156–1165.
Diary or Account of Siege, p.290.
Gentles, *New Model Army*, pp.283–285 and 300–314.
Hill, *Whose Who*, pp.130–134.
Brian Lyndon, 'Essex and the King's Cause' pp.26–39.
Manning, *1649*, p.47.
Underdown, *Purge*, p.357.
Walter, *Understanding Popular Violence*, p.336.
Wilson, *Fairfax*, p.153.

Chronology of National Events

1646

May:	King surrenders to Scots at Newark.
June:	End of Civil War with surrender of Royalist H.Q. at Oxford.
July:	Army complaints begin over pay arrears.

1647

February:	Parliament proposes reducing size of New Model Army.
March:	Army petition for redress of grievances dismissed by Parliament.
March–April:	Negotiations between Parliament and army at Saffron Walden.
May:	Parliament votes to disband army with only eight weeks of pay arrears.
June:	Army seizes King at Holdenby House.
July:	Army moves to Reading and presents *Heads of Proposals* treaty to King.
	Attempted counter-revolution by Presbyterians in London fails.
August:	New Model Army occupies London.
October:	Putney debates begin.
November:	King escapes from Hampton Court to Isle of Wight.
	Leveller mutiny in army at Ware crushed: some ringleaders shot.
December:	Charles rejects proposed treaty and makes Engagement with Scots.

1648

January:	Parliament passes Vote of No Addresses to the King.
March:	Revolt in Pembrokeshire against New Model Army.
April:	Army prayer meeting condemns Charles Stuart as 'That Man of Blood'.
	Rebellion in Wales spreads: Cromwell sent.

May:	Royalists rise in Kent and in the navy.
	Fairfax defeats rebels at Maidstone.
June:	Royalist rebellion in Essex: remnants of Kent rebels join them.
	Siege of Colchester begins.
July:	Scottish army of Engagement under Duke of Hamilton invades.
	South Wales rebels surrender to Cromwell at Pembroke.
August:	Scots defeated at Preston by Cromwell after long march from Wales.
	Colchester surrenders.
	Parliament revokes Vote of No Addresses.
September:	Parliament restarts negotiations with King at Newport, Isle of Wight.
November:	The Remonstrance of the Army calls for King to answer for his 'crimes'.
December:	New Model Army occupies London again.
	Commons votes to continue negotiations with King
	Parliament purged by Colonel Pride of Royalist-inclined MPs.

1649

January:	Trial and execution of the King.
February:	Leveller leaders arrested.
May:	England declared a republican Commonwealth.
	Levellers in army mutiny: suppressed by Cromwell and Fairfax.

Chronology of the Second Civil War, 1648

22 February:	Colonel Poyer refuses to yield Pembroke Castle to New Model Army.
3 March:	Tenby Castle in South Wales taken by Royalist rebels.
9–10 April:	Anti government riots in London.
24 April:	Riots in Norwich.
25 April:	Recruiting starts in Scotland for a Royalist Army of Engagement.
28–29 April:	Berwick and Carlisle fall to Royalist rebels.
8 May:	Riots in Bury St Edmunds.
	Rebels defeated in St Fagan's near Cardiff.
21–22 May:	Royalist rising in Kent.
27 May:	Naval mutiny against Parliament at the Downs in Kent.
31 May:	Tenby Castle retaken for Parliament.
1 June:	Kent rebels defeated at Maidstone.
3–4 June:	Royalists rise in Essex.
	Rebels at Chelmsford seize Parliament's County Committee.
	Dover Castle relieved by Parliament.
6 June:	Kent insurgents cross the Thames to rendezvous with Essex rebels.
9 June:	Naval mutineers sail their ships to Holland.
12 June:	Rebels enter Colchester.
	Royalist rising at Linton.
29 June:	Royalist rising at Horsham in Sussex.
5 July:	Earl of Holland leads rising at Kingston-upon-Thames.
8 July:	Scots army of Engagement crosses into England.
10 July:	Holland defeated at St Neots in Cambridgeshire.
11 July:	Poyer surrenders Pembroke Castle to Cromwell.
12 July:	Walmer Castle in Kent surrenders to Parliament.
22 July:	Prince of Wales arrives off Yarmouth.
13 August:	Scots finally move south through Lancashire.
	Sir Marmaduke Langdale moves to meet them at Preston.
14 August:	Attempted naval landing at Deal repulsed.
17 August:	Langdale and the Scots defeated by Cromwell at Preston.
19 August:	Remaining Scots mopped up at Winwick and Warrington.

25 August:	Duke of Hamilton surrenders at Uttoxeter.
	Langdale captured in Nottingham.
	Deal Castle in Kent surrenders to Parliament.
28 August:	Colchester surrenders.
3 September:	Prince of Wales's fleet returns to Holland.
8 September:	Remnants of Scots retreat north of the border.
	Cromwell backs anti-Royalist coup in Scotland.

Chronology of the Siege

9 June:	Advance guard of Royalist horsemen secure the town gates.
10 June:	Lord Norwich arrives with 5,600 horse and foot.
12 June:	Norwich begins to fortify Colchester.
	Fairfax arrives in the evening with advance guard.
13 June:	Fairfax attacks, penetrates Head Gate, but is repulsed.
14 June:	Fairfax digs in for a siege and sends for reinforcements.
17 June:	Lucas and 1,200 horsemen raid surrounding area for livestock and grain.
	Two Royalist ships land grain before being intercepted at sea.
18 June:	Fairfax refuses to deal with Lucas saying he cannot be trusted.
19 June:	Hope of early relief dashed when a Royalist rising at Linton is defeated.
20 June:	Siege tightens and first deserters leave garrison.
	Fairfax withdraws offer of quarter to officers: guarantees it only to men.
22 June:	Garrison sallies out in force to attack leaguer and search for food.
23 June:	First complaints of war crimes: garrison accused of using poisoned bullets.
2 July:	Colchester completely cut off.
5–11 July:	Senior Parliamentary officers killed in garrison raids.
	News reaches garrison of more Royalist defeats.
	Pembroke Castle surrenders to Cromwell.
15 July:	Goring threatens to hang any Parliamentary messengers offering amnesty.
	Attempted cavalry breakout foiled by treacherous local guides.
	Suburbs burned down by Parliamentary troops.
22 July:	Lord Capel's son is taken hostage.
	More complaints of poisoned bullets from Parliamentarians.
23 July:	Parliamentarians take the Hythe.
25 July:	Most defenders die as Abbey Gate magazine blows up.
	The Lucas home is overrun and sacked.
	St Mary at the Walls tower shelled and its artillery piece destroyed.
	Royalists suspect full-scale attack imminent.
	Parliamentary night attack repulsed.
26 July:	Garrison strengthens defensive weak points.

	Royalists fire houses near the town wall to deny Parliament snipers cover.
	More fires in the suburbs.
2 August:	Town reported in 'miserable condition': bad food spreads sickness.
7 August:	Antagonism increases between townspeople and garrison.
12 August:	Soldiers beat off civilians demanding food.
16 August:	Norwich promises surrender in twenty days if not relieved.
	Fairfax says he will be in the town long before then.
20 August:	Fairfax makes another offer of mercy to garrison rank and file.
21 August:	Gates opened so starving civilians can leave: Fairfax drives them back.
21–28 Aug:	News of Scots defeat reaches Colchester: new surrender terms are sought.
	Garrison troops mutiny.
28 August:	Colchester surrenders.
	Lucas and Lisle shot by firing squad.

BIBLIOGRAPHY

PRIMARY SOURCES

W.C. Abbott (ed.), *The Writings and Speeches of Oliver Cromwell* (Harvard 1937–1944).
R. Bell, *Memorials of the Civil War: Comprising the Correspondence of the Fairfax Family:* 2 vols (1819).
Calendar of State Papers, Domestic Series, of the Reign of Charles I, 1648–49.
W.D. Hamilton (ed.), *Calendar of State Papers, Domestic Series, 1648–49.*
H. Carey (ed.), *Memorials of the English Civil War 1646–1653:* 2 vols (London 1842).
Matthew Carter, *A True Relation of that Honourable, Though Unfortunate Expedition of Kent, Essex and Colchester in 1648: the second edition* (J. Fenno, Colchester, 1789, first published 1650).
Edward Earl of Clarendon, *The History of the Rebellion and Civil Wars in England*: 6 vols (reprint, 1819, Oxford 1843).
Colchester's Teares: Affecting & Afflicting City and Country: Dropping from the sad face of a New Wart threatening to bury in her own Ashes that woful town (John Bellamy, London, 1648).
Diary or Account of the Siege or Blockade of Colchester Anno 1648 (Historical MSS. Commission, 14th Report Appendix, Part 9), pp.281–290.
Daniel Defoe, *A Tour Through the Whole Island of Great Britain* (Penguin, 1979).
C.H. Firth (ed.), *A Selection of the Paper of William Clark, Secretary to the Council of the Army 1647–1649*, vol. 2 (Camden Society, 1894, reprinted 1965).
The Memoirs of Edmund Ludlow: 2 vols (London 1894).
William Haller & Godfrey Davies (eds) *The Leveller Tracts 1647–1653: Reprinted*, (Gloucester, Mass., 1964).
William Lilly, *History of his Life and Times from 1602–1681* (1751).
Thomas Taylor Lewis (ed.), *Letters of Brilliana Harley* (Camden Old Series, vol. 58, 1854).
A Narrative of the Siege of Colchester (Historical MSS Commission, 12th Report).
J. McFarlane (ed.) *Diary of Ralph Josselin 1616–1683* (British Academy Records of Social and Economic History, New Series, vol. III, 1976).
E. Hockliffe (ed.), *The Diary of the Rev. Ralph Josselin 1616–1683* (Royal Historical Society, 1908).
John Milton, 'Areopagitica (1644)', *Complete Prose Works of John Milton, Volume II 1643–1648* (New Haven, 1959), pp.480–570.
W.J.C. Moens (ed.), *Register of the Dutch Church, Colchester: Transactions of the Huguenot Society of London* (1905).
Ivan Roots (ed.), *Speeches of Oliver Cromwell* (Everyman, 1989).
John Rushworth, *Historical Collections*: vol. 4 (London: D. Browne, 1721–22)
George Thomason, *Calendar of the Thomason Tracts, 1640–1660, Vol. 1 & 2* (1908).
Thomason Tracts (Microfilm, Cambridge University Library).
Bulstrode Whitelock, *Memorials of the English Affairs; or An historical account of what passed from the beginning of the reign of King Charles the first, to King Charles the second, his happy restauration* (1682).
Don M. Wolfe (ed.), *Leveller Manifestoes of the Puritan Revolution: Reprinted* (London, 1967).
A.S.P. Woodhouse (ed.), *Puritanism and Liberty: Being the Army Debates 1647–49* (London, 1938).

SECONDARY SOURCES

J.S.A. Adamson, 'The English Nobility and the Projected Settlement of 1647', *Historical Journal*, No.30, 3 (1987).
David Appleby, *Our Fall, Our Fame* (Jacobus, 1996).
Robert Ashton, *Counter Revolution: The Second Civil War and its Origins 1646–8* (Yale, 1994).
'From Cavalier to Roundhead Tyranny, 1642–9', in John Morrill (ed.), *Reactions to the English Civil War, 1642–1649* (Macmillan, 1982).
The English Civil War: Conservatism and Revolution 1603–1649, Second Edition (Weidenfeld, 1989).
M. Atkin, *Gloucester and the Civil War: A City Under Siege* (Stroud, 1992).
G.E. Aylmer, *The Interregnum: The Quest for Settlement 1646–1660* (London, 1972).
'Crisis and Regrouping in the Political Elites: England from the 1630s to the 1660s', in J.G.A. Pocock(ed.), *Three British Revolutions: 1641, 1688, 1776* (Princeton, 1980).
M. Bennett, '"My plundered townes, my houses devastation": The Civil War and North Midlands Life', *Midland History*, No.22 (1997).
A.L. Beier, 'Vagrants and the Social Order in Elizabethan England', *Past and Present*, No.64 (1974).
H.N Brailsford, *The Levellers and the English Revolution* (Nottingham, 1976).
Robert Brenner, *Merchants and Revolution: Commercial Change, Political Conflict and London's Overseas Traders 1550–1653* (Cambridge, 1993).
'The Civil War Politics of London's Merchant Community', *Past & Present*, No.58 (1973)
J. Burk, 'The New Model Army and the Problems of Siege Warfare, 1648-51', *Irish Historical Studies*, vol. XXVII, No.105 (May, 1990).
Mark Byford, 'The Birth of a Protestant Town: the Process of Reformation in Tudor Colchester, 1530–80', in Patrick Collinson and John Craig (eds), *The Reformation of English Towns 1500–1640: Themes in Focus* (Macmillan, 1998).
Bernard Capp, *Cromwell's Navy: The Fleet and the English Revolution 1648–1660* (Oxford, 1989).
'The Fifth Monarchists and Popular Millenarianism', in J.F. McGregor and B. Reay (eds), *Radical Religion in the English Revolution* (Oxford, 1984).
Norah Carlin, '"Liberty and Fraternities in the English Revolution: The Politics of London Artisans" Protests 1635–1659"', *International Review of Social History*, No.39 (1994).
Charles Carlton, *Going to the Wars: The Experience of the British Civil Wars, 1638–1651* (Routledge, 1994).
David T. and D. Clarke, *The Siege of Colchester 1648* (Cultural Activities Committee, Colchester Borough Council).
J.T. Cliffe, *Puritans in Conflict: The Puritan Gentry During and After the Civil Wars* (London, 1998).
Norman Cohn, *Pursuit of the Millennium* (Oxford, 1970).
Will Coster, 'Fear and Friction in Urban Communities During the English Civil War', in William G. Naphy and Penny Roberts (eds), *Fear in Early Modem Society* (Manchester, 1997).
Barry Coward, *Oliver Cromwell: Profiles in Power* (Longman, 1994, fourth impression).
The Stuart Age, England 1603–1714 (Longman, 1994, second edition). Richard Cust and Ann Hughes (eds), *Conflict in Early Stuart England: Studies in Religion and Politics 1603–1642* (Longman, 1994).
J.C. Davis, *Oliver Cromwell: Reputations* (Arnold, 2001).
J.R. Davis, *Thesis on Colchester Borough Administration 1600–1660* (Brandeis University, USA, early 1980s).
B. Donagan, 'Prisoners in the English Civil War', *History Today*, No.41 (March, 1991).
'Atrocity, War Crime and Treason in the English Civil War', *American Historical Review*,

vol. 99, No.4 (October, 1994).
F.D. Dow, *Radicalism in the English Revolution 1640–1660* (Oxford, 1985).
Jacqueline Eales, *Puritans and Roundhead: The Harleys of Brampton Bryan and the Outbreak of the English Civil War* (Cambridge, 1990).
C.H. Firth, *Cromwell's Army: A History of the English Soldier During the Civil Wars, the Commonwealth and the Protectorate, being the Ford Lectures Delivered to the University of Oxford 1900–1901* (Methuen, 1962).
Anthony Fletcher, *A County Community in Peace and War: Sussex 1600–1660* (London, 1975).
S.R. Gardiner, *History of the Great Civil War, 1642–1649.*, vol. I, (1893).
Ian Gentles, *The New Model Army in England, Ireland and Scotland 1645–1653* (Oxford, 1992).
'The Struggle for London in the Second Civil War', *The Historical Journal*, vol. XXVI (1983).
'Arrears of Pay and Ideology in the Army Revolt of 1647', in Brian Bond and Ian Roy (eds), *War and Society*: vol. 1 (1976).
John Morrill and Blair Worden (eds), *Soldiers, Writers and Statesmen of the English Revolution* (Cambridge, 1998).
G.P. Gooch, *English Democratic Ideas in the Seventeenth Century* (Cambridge, 1927).
Richard Gough, *The History of Middle* (Caliban, 1979).
Paul Griffiths, Adam Fox and Steve Hindle, *The Experience of Authority in Early Modem England* (Macmillan, 1996).
Christopher Hibbert, *Cavaliers and Roundheads: The English War 1642–1649* (HarperCollins, 1994).
Derek Hirst, *Authority and Conflict: England 1603–1658* (London, 1986).
Christopher Hill, *The World Turned Upside Down: Radical Ideas during the English Revolution* (Penguin, 1991).
Puritanism and Revolution (London, 1958).
'A Bourgeois Revolution?', in J.G.A. Poeock (ed.), *Three British Revolutions: 1641, 1688, 1776* (Princeton, 1980).
A Nation of Change and Novelty: Radical Politics, Religion and Literature in Seventeenth Century England (London, 1990).
Christopher Hill & Edmund Dell (eds), *The Good Old Cause: Documents of the English Revolution of 1640–1660: Its Causes, Course and Consequences* (Augustus Kelley, 1969).
C.P. Hill, *Whose Who in Smart England* (Shepheard-Walwyn, 1988).
Ann Hughes, *The Causes of the English Civil War* (Macmillan, 1994).
Politics, Society and Civil War in Warwickshire, 1620–1660 (Cambridge, 1987).
William Hunt, *The Puritan Moment: The Coming of Revolution to an English County* (Harvard, 1983)
Ronald Hutton, *The British Republic, 1649 - 1660* (London, 1975).
Sybil M. Jack, *Towns in Tudor and Stuart Britain: Social History in Perspective* (Macmillan, 1996).
Edwin Jones, *The English Nation: The Great Myth*, (Sutton, 2000), chapter II, p.61–93.
Jack D. Jones, *The Royal Prisoner* (Carisbrooke Castle Museum, Lutterworth, 1965 and 1974).
John Kenyon (ed.) *The Smart Constitution 1603–1688: Documents and Commentary* (Cambridge, 1978)
John Kenyon and Jane Ohlmeyer (eds) *The Civil Wars: A Military History of England, Scotland and Ireland 1638–1660* (Oxford, 1998).
Mark Kishlansky, *A Monarchy Transformed: Britain 1603-1714* (Allen Lane, 1996).
The Rise of the New Model Army (Cambridge, 1979).
Mark A. Kishlansky, 'The Army and the Levellers: The Road to Putney', *The Historical Journal*, vol. XVII (1979).
'Ideology and Politics in the Parliamentary Armies 1645–49', in J.S. Morrill, *Reactions to the English Civil War 1642–1649* (London, 1982).

Frank Kitson, *Prince Rupert: Portrait of a Soldier* (Constable, 1994), p.14–27.
Prince Rupert: Admiral and General-at-Sea (Constable 1999).
R.W. Ketton-Cremer, *Norfolk in the Civil War* (Gliddon, 1985).
K. Lindley, 'Riot Prevention and Control in Early Stuart London', *Transactions of the Royal Historical Society*, 5th series, XXXIII (1983).
Keith Lindley, 'London and Popular Freedom in the 1640s', in R.C. Richardson and G.M. Ridden (eds), *Freedom in the English Revolution: Essays in History and Literature* (Manchester, 1986).
B.P. Lyndon, 'Essex and the King's Cause in 1648', *Historical Journal*, XXIX (1956).
Alan Macfarlane, *The Origins of English Individualism: The Family, Property and Social Transition* (Oxford, 1978).
Michael Mahony, 'Presbyterianism in the City of London', *The Historical Journal*, vol. XXII (1979).
Brian Manning, *1649: The Crisis of the English Revolution* (Bookmarks, 1992).
The English People and the English Revolution (London, 1976).
Aristocrats, Plebians and Revolution in England 1640–1660 (Pluto, 1996).
Clements R. Markham, Life *of the Great Lord Fairfax* (Macmillan, 1870).
J. Mather, 'The Moral Code of the English Civil War and the Interregnum', *Historian*, vol. 44, No.3 (May, 1982).
Derek Massarella, 'The Politics of the Army and the Quest for Settlement', in Ivan Roots (ed.), *Into Another Mould: Aspects of the Interregnum: Exeter Studies in History No.3* (Exeter, 1981).
Patrick Morrah, *Prince Rupert of the Rhine* (Constable, 1976), pp.213–241.
John Morrill, *Revolt in the Provinces: The People of England and the Tragedies of War 1630–1648* (Penguin, 1999).
The Nature of the English Revolution: Essays (Longman, 1993).
'Mutiny and Discontent in the English Provincial Armies 1645–1647', *Past & Present*, No.56 (1972).
(ed.), The *Scottish National Covenant in its British Context 1638–51* (Edinburgh, 1990).
Valerie Pearl, *London and the Outbreak of the Puritan Revolution* (Oxford, 1964).
'London's Counter Revolution', in G.E. Aylmer (ed.), *The Interregnum: The Quest for Settlement 1646–1660: first reprint* (Macmillan, 1990).
S. Porter, *Destruction in the English Civil Wars* (Stroud, 1994).
R.C. Richardson & G.M. Ridden (eds), *Freedom in the English Revolution: Essays in History and Literature* (Manchester, 1986).
R.C. Richardson (ed.), *Town and Countryside in the English Revolution* (Manchester, 1992).
Jasper Ridley, *The Roundheads* (Constable, 1976).
Penny Roberts, 'Agencies Human and Divine: Fire in French Cities, 1520–1720', in William G. Naphy and Penny Roberts (eds), *Fear in Early Modern Society* (Manchester, 1997).
I. Roy, 'England Turned, Germany? The Aftermath of the Civil War in its European Context', *Transactions of the Royal Historical Society*, 5th Series, XXVIII (1978).
J.H. Round, 'Colchester During the Commonwealth', *English Historical Review, No.15* (1900).
E.J. Rudsdale, *'A hitherto unrecorded incident in the siege of Colchester: Capt. James Hinde the highwayman'* (Essex County Standard, 18 June 1927).
Conrad Russell (ed.), *The Origins of the English Civil War* (Macmillan, 1991).
'The British Problem and the English Civil War', *History*, vol. 72 (1987).
S.R. Smith, 'Almost Revolutionaries: The London Apprentices During the Civil Wars', *The Huntingdon Library Quarterly*, XLII (1978–9).
Lawrence Stone, *The Causes of the English Revolution: 1529–1642* (Routledge, 1972).
'Social Mobility in England 1500–1700', *Past & Present*, No.33 (1966).
'The Results of the English Revolution', in J.G.A. Pocock (ed.), *Three British Revolutions: 1641, 1688, 1776* (Princeton, 1980).

Mark Stoyle, *From Deliverance to Destruction: Rebellion and Civil War in an English City* (Exeter, 1996).
Loyalty and Locality: Popular Allegiance in Devon during the English Civil War (Exeter, 1994).
Barbara Taft, 'The Council of Officers' Agreement of the People 1648–49', *The Historical Journal*, vol. XXVIII (1985).
Keith Thomas, *Religion and the Decline of Magic* (Penguin, 1991).
Revd Geo. Fyler Townsend, *The Siege of Colchester; or An Event of the Civil War AD 1648* (London, 1881).
David Underdown, *Pride's Purge: Politics in the Puritan Revolution* (Oxford, 1971).
Revel, Riot and Rebellion: Popular Politics and Culture in England 1603–1660 (Oxford, 1987).
'Chalk and Cheese: Contrasts Among the English Clubmen', *Past & Present*, No.85 (1979).
John Walter, *Understanding Popular Violence in the English Revolution: The Colchester Plunderers* (Cambridge, 1999).
C.V. Wedgwood, *The Trial of King Charles I* (Penguin, 1983).
Peter Wenham, *The Siege of York, 1644* (Sessions, 1994).
John Wilson, *Fairfax: A Life of Thomas, Lord Fairfax, Captain General of all the Parliament's Forces in the English Civil War and Creator and Commander of the New Model Army* (Murray, 1985).
Don M. Wolfe, *Milton in the Puritan Revolution* (London, 1941).
Andy Wood, *Riot Rebellion and Popular Politics in Early Modern England* (Palgrave, 2002).
Austin Woolrych, *The Battles of the English Civil War* (Batsford, 1961).
Soldiers and Statesmen: The General Council of the Army and Its Debates 1647–1648 (Oxford, 1987).
Blair Worden, *The Rump Parliament 1648–1653* (Cambridge, 1974),
Daphne Woodward and Chloe Cockerill, *The Siege of Colchester 1648: A History and a Bibliography: 2nd revised edition* (Essex County Library, 1979).
John Wright, 'Highwayman Who Served in the Great Siege', *Essex County Standard* (5 Sept 1952).
Keith Wrightson and David Levine, *Poverty and Piety in an English Village: Terling 1525–1700* (New York, 1979).
Susan Yaxley (ed.), *The Siege of King's Lynn 1643: A briefe and true Relation of the Siege and Surrendering of Kings Lyn to the Earle of Manchester* (Larks Press, 1993).
P. Young, 'Major Jammot, Adjutant General, an unknown hero of the Siege of Colchester', *Essex Review*, vol. LVII.
Perez Zagorin, *Rebels and Rulers, 1500–1660: Volume II, Provincial Rebellion Revolutionary Civil Wars, 1560–1660* (Cambridge, 1982).

LIST OF ILLUSTRATIONS

Unless otherwise stated pictures are from the author's collection.

1. The Keymer Map of the siege of Colchester. Essex County Council.
2. Prince Rupert of the Rhine.
3. Lieutenant-General Oliver Cromwell.
4. Sir Thomas Fairfax, Commander-in-Chief of the New Model Army.
5. Fairfax presides at army council meeting. Essex County Council.
6. Sir Harbottle Grimston. Colchester Museums.
7. Sir Marmaduke Langdale.
8. The Home Counties and East Anglia, showing some of the main trouble spots in the Second Civil War of 1648.
9. Kent Report. Essex County Council.
10. Sir Charles Lucas. Colchester Museums.
11. Sir George Lisle. Colchester Museums.
12. Reports of the first battle at Colchester. Essex County Council.
13. The site of the old Head Gate at Colchester as it looks today.
14. Sir Thomas Honywood. Essex County Council.
15. Bastion at Colchester.
16. The Hythe. Essex County Council.
17. Mersea Fort.
18. *Colchester Teares*. Essex County Council.
19. Charles, Prince of Wales.
20. Major-General John Lambert.
21. The tower of St Mary's at the Walls.
22. Siege House.
23. Siege House bullet holes.
24. Siege House bullet holes.
25. From the Leaguer. Essex County Council.
26. Explosion at the Lucas's family home. Essex County Council.
27. Abbey Gate.
28. Cannon damage to the Abbey Gate.
29. St Mary's Tower.
30. Sir Thomas Fairfax with a specimen of his signature.
31. Royalist Propaganda. Essex County Council.
32.–34. Allegations of war crimes. Essex County Council.
35. Fire. Essex County Council.
36. Section of St John's which was set on fire.
37. Capel kidnapping. Essex County Council.
38. Edmund Ludlow.
39. Hope of Langdale relief. Essex County Council.
40. Naval mutiny. Essex County Council.
41. Prince of Wales at Yarmouth. Essex County Council.
42. Prince Charles's declaration. Essex County Council.
43. Oliver Cromwell.
44. The original document surrendering Colchester. Essex County Council.
45. The surrender reported. Essex County Council.
46. The siege seen through the eyes of a serving officer. Essex County Council.
47. The Old King's Head.
48. Sir Bernard Gascoigne. Colchester Museums.
49. Colchester Castle.
50. Loyal sacrifice of Sir Charles Lucas and Sir George Lisle. Colchester County Museums.
51. Memorial to Lucas and Lisle.
52. Sir Thomas Fairfax's explanation of the Lucas and Lisle executions. Essex County Council.
53. Elegies to Lucas and Lisle. Essex County Council.
54. Matthew Carter's account of the siege. Essex County Council.
55. Lady Anne Fairfax.
56. Signatories to King Charles's death-warrant.
57. Lord Capel. Colchester Museums.
58. William Lenthall.
59. St Botolph's Priory.
60. Blown up walls
61. Monument inscription.
62. Tombstone.
63. Cromwell with crowns.
64. Sir Thomas Fairfax.
65. *Eikon Basilike* – the image of Charles I as martyr.

INDEX

A Dangerous and Bloudy Plot Discovered; 143.
A Discovery of the Intentions of the Army; 108.
Abbey Gate; 82–84.
abduction; see atrocities.
Act of Indemnity; 80.
agitators; 25, 28, 150.
Agreement of the People; 26, 151.
agriculture; 31.
ammunition; see supplies.
amnesty; see parole.
Amsterdam; 71.
Anglican Church; 14, 38.
apprentices; 25.
arson; see fire.
Articles of War; 106.
Arundel; 147.
Ashburnham, John; 24.
assault; see atrocities.
astrology; 121–122.
atrocities; 20, 92, 97–98, 102–104, 111, 123, 143.
Axtell, Lt Col Daniel; 154–155.
Aylesford; 45.

ballads; see propaganda.
Barbados; 147.
Barksted, Col; 43.
Barksted's Fort; 74, 78.
Barrington, Sir Thomas; 32.
Bastwick, John; 32.
Batten, Vice Admiral William; 37, 114.
batteries; see fortifications.
Berkshire; 24.
Berry Fields; 125.
Berwick; 39–40.
Blackheath; 45.
Book of Common Prayer; 15, 38.
Booker, John; 121–122.
Bradshaw, John; 155–156, 158.
bread; see supplies.
Brecon; 38.
Brentwood; 55.
Bristol; 10.
Buckingham, Duke of; 67–68, 164.
bullets, poisoned and dum-dum; see atrocities.
Burford; 164.
Burton, Henry; 32.
Bury St Edmunds; 36.

Calvinism; 29, 71.
Cambridgeshire; 53, 57, 71, 113.
Canterbury; 41.
Capel, Lady; 102, 104, 133.
Capel, Lord; 48, 50, 52–53, 71–72, 91, 102–103, 113, 140, 157–160.
capitalism; 17.
Cardiff; 147.
Carisbrooke Castle; 28, 147.
Carlisle; 39–40, 110, 122.
Carter, Matthew, Quartermaster General; 50, 53, 57–59, 76, 78, 84–85, 87–92, 99, 102, 111, 112, 120, 125–128, 130–133, 137, 139–140, 143, 145–146, 157–158, 161, 170.
Castle, of Colchester; 135–137, 139, 141, 163, 165.
Catholics; 15–16, 32.
cats and dogs; see famine.
Cavaliers; 17, 36, 39, 43, 45, 48, 59, 63–65, 89, 91, 105, 119, 132, 148.
cavalry; 18, 55, 81, 87–89, 91, 106, 111, 113, 122–123, 128, 131, 135, 151.
censorship; 93, 95–96.
Channel, the; 68.
Charing Cross; 151, 156.
Charles II; 50, 69, 166, 168–169.
Chatham; 41.
Chelmsford; 48–50, 102, 104.
Chepstow; 40.
Christmas; 16, 24, 41.
circumvallation; see fortifications.
civilians; 18, 20, 28, 30, 32, 43, 80–81, 88–93, 97, 105, 108, 117, 119, 123, 126, 130, 132, 149.
Clarendon, Earl of; 48, 50, 114.
Clarke, William; 135, 137.
class; 10, 11, 17, 22, 106.
Colchester Spie; 94, 97, 103.
Colchester Teares; 64–65, 97, 101, 121.
Colchester; 9–12, 18, 31–34, 36, 45–50, 52–54, 55–57, 59–60, 63–65, 67–69, 71–74,

76–82, 87–88, 90–92, 97–100, 102–103, 105, 107–108, 110, 112–114, 115, 118–125, 127–132, 135, 139, 142–142, 144–147, 157–164, 170.
Colne, River; 58, 62–63, 74, 115.
commissions of the peace; 37.
Commonwealth; 35, 79, 154, 160, 164.
composition; 142, 149.
Cooke, Mayor William; 89.
corn; see supplies.
Cornwall; 147.
corruption; 35.
Cotswolds; 164.
county committees; 35, 48, 92, 102–104.
coup d'état; 11, 25, 107–108, 125, 152.
Covenant and the Covenanters; 23–24, 29, 40, 70, 119, 122.
Coventry; 73.
Cromwell, Oliver; 14, 19–20, 22, 26, 28–29, 40, 65–67, 72–74, 112, 123–125, 135, 143, 150, 152–156, 158–159, 163–164, 166–167, 169.
Cumberland; 123.

Dartford; 41.
Deal; 41, 74, 114–115, 119.
death march; 146.
defences; see fortifications.
Defoe, Daniel; 161.
Deptford; 41.
Derby House Committee; 41, 67, 142, 144.
Derbyshire; 73.
desertion; 58, 64, 76, 91, 112.
diarist, of Colchester; 49, 54, 78, 85, 89–91, 112, 113, 126–127.
disease; 10, 19, 59, 89, 130.
Doncaster; 143.
Dorset; 67.
Dover; 43, 48.
Downs, the; 37, 41, 74, 78, 113, 115.
Dutch; 19, 32, 68, 116, 119, 161.

earthworks; see fortifications.
East Anglia; 9, 24, 31–32, 36, 41, 69, 115.
East Bridge; 63, 74.
East Gate, 128.
East Street; 76–77.
East Ward; 161.
Eikon Basilike; 169.
elections; 26.
Elizabeth, Queen; 157.
Engagement and the Engagers; 29, 40, 61, 65, 69–70, 112, 122–124.
epidemics; see disease.
episcopacy; 14–15, 32.
Epping; 55.
Essex; 10, 31–32, 34–36, 48–49, 55–58, 68, 71, 102–106, 142, 163.
Europe; 16, 18, 31, 100, 135.
Evelyn, John; 161.
Ewers, Col; 74, 106, 133.
executions; 11, 72, 130, 134–135, 137–139, 140–143, 145, 150, 152, 156–158, 163–166, 168.
extortion; 20.

fair quarter; 129.
Fairfax, Lady Anne; 154–155, 164.
Fairfax, Sir Thomas also Lord; 12, 18, 20–21, 24–27, 38, 40–41, 44–47, 49–50, 53–59, 61–64, 66, 71–74, 81, 88–90, 98, 101, 104–110, 113, 118, 121, 125–132, 135, 137, 141–144, 151–156, 158, 164, 166, 168–169.
famine; 10, 19, 36, 53, 55, 80–81, 89, 91–92, 125–126, 132, 140, 145–147, 149–150.
Farre, Col; 133.
fifth column; 88.
Fight, A; 105.
fine; 132, 161.
fire; 10, 19, 53, 87, 99, 100–102.
firing squad; see executions.
fleet; see navy.
Florence; 135.
fluxes; see disease.
fodder; see supplies.
food; see supplies.
forage; see supplies.
fortifications; 12, 38, 53, 58–59, 61, 63, 72, 74, 78, 82, 85, 87, 125–126, 131–132, 161, 163.
forts; see fortifications.
France and the French; 23, 30, 39, 43, 67–68, 100, 116.
franchise; 26, 37.
French Revolution; 93.
Fryer's Yard; 128.

Gascoigne, Bernard aka Bernardo Guasconi; 133–135, 139–140.
Gate House; 82–84.
Geneva; 71.
Glamorgan; 38, 66.
Gloucester; 67, 147.
Gloucestershire; 137.
Goldsmith's Hall; 142.
grain; see supplies.
Grand Duke, of Tuscany; 135.
Grandees; 26, 28–29, 164.
Gravesend; 49.
Great Blow, at Norwich; 36.
Greenwich; 45, 50.
Grey, Thomas; 156.

Grimston, Harbottle; 32–33, 74.
gunpowder, see supplies.

Hamilton, Duke of; 74, 122, 123, 130, 154, 157.
Hammond, Col; 143.
Hampshire; 67.
Hampton Court; 28.
harvests; 20, 58, 149.
Harwich; 62, 115.
Hatfield Broad Oak, or Hatfield Brodock; 106.
Head Gate; 52–53.
Head Street; 53, 133.
Head Ward; 161.
Helvoetsluys; 119.
Henrietta Maria, Queen; 23, 67, 148
Henry VIII; 34.
Hereford; 147.
Hertfordshire; 24, 28, 48, 67.
High Court of Justice; 154, 160
High Street; 53
Highlands; 24
Hobbes, Thomas; 45.
Holland, Earl of; 67, 113, 157.
Holland; 39, 115, 119, 168–169.
Holmby House; 24–25.
Home Counties; 35-36, 41, 43–44, 72.
Honywood, Sir Thomas; 49, 56–57.
Hopton, Sir Ralph; 18.
horseflesh; see famine.
Horsemander, Capt.; 82.
horses; see cavalry.
Horton, Col; 66–67.
hostages; see atrocities.
House of Commons; 11, 14, 20, 24–25, 29, 41, 108, 142, 144, 157–158, 160.
House of Lords; 26, 108, 157.
Hudson, Doctor; 24.
human shields; see atrocities.
Humpty Dumpty; 86–87.
hunger; see famine.
Huntingdon; 67–68.
Hurst Castle; 151.
Hyde Park; 55, 151.
Hythe, the; 61–62, 76, 82.

Independents; 14, 22, 68, 70, 120, 148, 163.
infantry; see soldiers.
inhabitants; see civilians.
Interregnum; 161, 164, 168.
Ireland and Irish; 19, 25, 43, 65, 70, 100, 166–167.
Ireton, Henry; 26, 59, 109, 135–136, 140, 150–152, 157–158, 160.
Isle of Wight; 118.
Isle of Wight; 28, 29, 40, 48, 143, 147.

James I, King; 157.
James, Duke of York; 29–30.
Jericho; 166–167.
journalists; 93.
Joyce, Col George; 25.
Julius Caesar; 59.
justice; 10, 105, 135–137, 140–141, 152–153, 155.

Kent; 37, 41, 43–44, 48–51, 74, 78, 113, 115.
kidnapping; see atrocities.
Killigrew, Lady; 85.
King Charles I; 9, 11, 13–14, 16–17, 19, 23–25, 28–29, 34–40, 43, 45, 54, 65, 67–72, 74, 78, 94–97, 100, 102, 104, 107–110, 113, 115–116, 119, 122–123, 130, 135, 137, 139, 142–144, 147–148, 150–158, 163–164, 168–169.
King's Head; 129, 133.
Kingdomes Weekly Intelligencer; 118, 126.
Kings Lynn, Lynn; 147.
Kingston-upon-Thames; 67, 113.
Kirk, the; 40, 70, 122, 124.

Lambert, Maj. Gen. John; 72–74, 122–123, 143.
Lambeth; 157.
Lancashire; 71, 123.
Langdale, Sir Marmaduke; 39, 71–72, 91, 110–111, 122–123.
Laud, Archbishop; 32.
Laugharne, Maj. Gen. Rowland; 38, 66–67, 72.
leaguer; 55, 57, 59, 76, 78, 83, 98, 106, 109, 111–112, 121, 125, 127, 132.
Leeds; 123.
Leicester; 73.
Leicestershire; 67, 73.
Lentall, William; 158, 160
Levellers; 26, 28, 41, 96, 114, 148–151, 164.
Lexden; 50, 53, 65, 74.
Lilly, William; 121–122.
Limerick; 59.
Lincolnshire; 24, 67, 71.
Linton; 57, 67.
Lisle, Sir George; 11, 47–48, 72, 76, 130, 132–141, 143–144, 158, 163, 165–166.
literacy; 94.
Lollards; 32.
London, 12, 14, 25–26, 31–32, 43–45, 48, 50, 53, 55, 57, 59, 68–69, 71, 95–96, 100, 109–110, 118, 121, 130, 139, 142, 148, 151, 161, 164.
Long Parliament, 32.
looting; see plunder.

Lord Protector; 164.
Loughborough, Lord; 78, 133.
Low Countries; 32.
Lucas, Lady; 85.
Lucas, Sir Charles; 11, 46–48, 49–50, 63, 72, 76, 82, 85, 88, 90, 97, 102, 113, 115, 121, 130, 133–145, 158, 163, 164–166.
Lucas, Sir John; 34, 48, 164.
Ludlow, Edmund; 45, 107.
Lymington, 151.

Magdeburg; 18.
Maidstone; 43, 48, 50–51, 53, 115
Maldon Road; 78.
Maldon; 74.
malnutrition; see famine.
Manchester, Earl of; 20, 140.
Marston Moor; 63–64, 142–143.
martial law; 108.
martyrdom; 142–143, 145, 166, 169.
Mary Tudor, Queen Mary I, 32.
Masham, Sir William; 102–104.
mass murder; see atrocities.
Maynard, Lord; 32.
Mazarin, Cardinal of France; 23.
media; see propaganda.
Mercurius Anglicus; 110.
Mercurius Bellicus; 68, 102, 105, 121.
Mercurius Britannicus; 101, 119, 122.
Mercurius Elencticus; 58, 104, 106, 117.
Mercurius Melancholicus; 88, 101, 117.
Mercurius Pragmaticus; 109.
Mercurius Psitacus, The Parrotting Mercury; 96, 101–102, 104, 110.
mercy; 129.
Mersea Island; 62–63.
Middle Mill; 78, 89.
Middle Mill; 87, 112.
Mile End; 74.
Militia Ordinance; 32.
Milton, John; 95.
Moderate Intelligencer, 91, 98–99, 101.
Moderate; 81, 96–97, 101, 132, 148.
moderates; 23, 66, 70, 108, 150–151.
monarchy; 13, 23, 26, 29, 34–35, 37, 105, 108, 116, 147, 150, 154, 161, 163, 169, 170.
Monck, Gen.; 169.
mutiny; 25, 37, 41, 72, 113–115, 118, 120, 127–128, 164.

Naseby, battle of; 20.
navy; 33, 37, 41, 43, 62, 68–69, 74, 113–120, 126, 149.
Nayland Bridge; 111.
Needham, Col; 53.
Netherlands; 31, 59.
neutrality; 118.
New Model Army; 10, 12, 17–22, 24–27, 29–30, 35–38, 40, 44–45, 50, 53, 59–62, 65–66, 68, 71–73, 80, 85, 89, 97, 105, 108, 114–115, 122–124, 130–131, 147, 168.
Newark, 23–24.
Newbury, battle of; 67.
Newcastle; 24, 29,
Newmarket; 25.
newsbooks; see propaganda.
newspapers; see propaganda.
Norfolk; 48, 57, 116.
North Gate; 63.
North Sea; 68.
North Ward; 161.
north, the; 122.
Northampton; 73.
Norwich, Earl of formerly Lord Goring; 43, 45, 50, 64, 78, 87, 89, 97–98, 102, 113, 115, 121, 126, 128, 133, 140, 157–158, 160.
Norwich; 36, 91.
Nottingham; 73, 123.
Nottinghamshire; 23, 67, 73.

officers; 17, 26, 28, 43, 53, 84, 91, 98, 106, 113, 120, 123, 125–128, 130, 133, 140, 146, 151.
Oxford; 23–24, 34, 67, 74, 147.

pamphlets; see propaganda.
Paris; 23.
Parliament; 9, 10, 13–14, 17, 20, 22–25, 29, 34–41, 43–45, 48, 54, 56–58, 66–70, 72, 74, 78, 80, 92, 95–96, 102–110, 113, 115, 117–118, 120–122, 124, 129–131, 135–136, 140, 142–144, 147–149, 151–152, 154, 157–158, 164, 169.
Parliament's Vulture; 70.
Parliamentary Kite or *Telltale Bird*; 35, 68, 98–99, 105, 122.
Parliamentary movement and Parliamentarians; 21, 30, 32, 35, 39, 44, 46, 55, 57, 62, 64, 66, 73, 78, 86, 88, 95, 97–99, 102, 104, 108, 110–111, 118–122, 135, 137, 146, 161, 164.
Parliaments Scritch-Owle, 95.
parole; 10, 63, 78, 113, 119, 120, 127, 142, 145.
pay, of the army and its arrears; 14, 20, 22, 24–25, 30, 38, 80, 105, 118, 149, 151.
Pembroke; 38, 40, 66–67, 72.
Pendennis; 147.
Perfect Weekly Account; 101.
Perfect Weekly Account; 73, 104.
Personal Rule of Charles I; 32.
Peterborough, Earl of; 67.

petitioning; 36.
pillage; see plunder.
plague; 163.
plunder; 17, 18, 20, 85, 105, 108, 123, 132, 146, 163.
Pontefract; 143, 150, 152, 153.
Pope; 16.
Popish Plot; 13, 16.
population; see civilians.
Portsmouth; 74, 115, 118.
Powell, Col Rice; 72.
Poyer, Col John; 37–38, 66–67, 72.
Prayer Book; see Book of Common Prayer.
Presbyterians; 14, 22–25, 29, 69, 93, 109, 119, 147–148.
Preston; 123–125, 127.
Pride, Col; 143, 152.
Pride's Purge; 152–153.
Prince of Orange; 39, 59.
Prince of Wales; 29, 38, 68–70, 74, 113–119, 121, 144.
Priory Street; 60.
prisoners; 53, 55, 76, 78, 98–99, 103, 128–129, 131, 135, 140, 143–145, 157–158.
prisons; 147.
privateering, 68.
propaganda; 35, 48, 59, 64–65, 92–97, 101–102, 105–106, 108, 110, 115, 119–121, 132, 138, 141–143, 145, 148, 150.
Protectorate; 169.
provisions; see supplies.
Prynne, William; 32.
purge, of House of Commons; 150.
Puritans; 16, 32, 34, 36, 94, 161.
Putney; 26, 28, 41.

quarter; 136, 143.
Queen Street; 151.

radicals; 11, 28–29, 37, 70, 108–109, 147–149, 151, 153, 164.
rain; see weather.
Rainsborough, Thomas; 26, 41, 74, 87, 114, 126, 137, 143.
ramparts; see fortifications.
rank and file; see soldier.
rape; see atrocities.
redoubts; see fortifications.
Reformation; 16, 32.
regicide; 151.
Republicans; 107, 109, 154, 164.
Restoration, the; 161, 163, 165-166.
revolution; 11, 13, 26-28, 30, 40, 109, 144, 147, 151–152, 164, 166.
Richard Baxter; 93.
Richmond, Duke of; 43.
riot; see civilians.
Rochester; 41.
Rochester; 43, 45.
Rome; 16.
Roundheads; 17, 72, 99, 101, 120, 163.
Royalists; 9–12, 17, 20, 22–24, 29–30, 32, 34–41, 43–46, 50, 53–55, 59–62, 64–66, 68, 70–74, 79, 85–86, 88, 93–96, 98, 102–106, 110, 112–119, 121, 123–124, 126, 128–133, 138, 140, 142–145, 149–150, 153, 157, 159–161, 163, 165–166, 169–170.
Rump; 157.
Rupert, Prince of the Rhine; 18.
Rushworth, John; 108, 126, 131.
Rutland; 67.
Rye Gate; 87.

sailors, see navy.
Saints; 16, 22, 59, 65, 85, 97–98, 105, 118, 147.
Salisbury; 164.
Sandwich; 74, 114.
Sawbridgeworth, 106.
Saye and Sele, Lord; 143.
Scotland and the Scots; 10, 19, 23–24, 28–29, 39–40, 43, 48, 59, 61, 65, 67, 69–74, 98, 110, 112, 119–120, 122–125, 127, 130, 143, 147, 152, 154, 157, 166–169.
Scott, Lady Katherine; 92.
Scroope, Col, 68.
sea; see navy.
Self Denying Ordinance; 20.
Sexby, Edward; 26.
Shakespeare; 15.
Shambrook, Col, 98.
Sheffield, Mr Sampson; 104.
Ship Money; 34.
ships; see navy.
Short Parliament; 32.
shortages; see famine.
Shropshire; 73.
Siege House; 76–77.
siegeworks; see fortifications.
slaves; 147.
soldiers, private, rank and file, other ranks; 10, 18–20, 22, 25–26, 28, 35, 43, 48, 53, 58, 78, 87, 89–90, 98, 105–106, 113–114, 119, 120, 125–128, 130, 135–137, 144–147, 150–151, 154, 161, 164.
Solent; 151.
South Ward; 161.
Southwell; 24.
Spain and the Spanish; 59.
Speaker, House of Commons; 144, 158.
Speaker, House of Lords; 140.
Spragg, the Rev.; 143.

St Leger, Sir Anthony; 115, 119.
St Albans; 26, 151.
St Botolph's Priory; 162.
St Fagan's; 67.
St. Giles's Church; 163–164, 166.
St James's Church; 128.
St John's Abbey; 34, 82.
St John's; 100.
St Mary's at the Walls Church; 74–75, 85–87, 128, 161, 163.
St Michael's Mount; 147.
St Neot's; 68, 157.
Staffordshire; 130.
starvation; see famine.
Stephens, Edward; 156.
Stinchcombe; 137.
stores; see supplies.
suburbs; 53, 87, 101.
Suffolk; 34, 36, 48, 57-58, 111.
supplies; 19, 31, 57–58, 62, 71–72, 74, 76, 78–79, 81–82, 87, 89–91, 105–106, 122–123, 125, 127–128, 149.
surrender; 10, 23, 63, 90, 108, 113, 125, 128–132, 145.
Surrey; 36, 67.
Sussex; 67.

taxation; 14, 20, 30, 35–36, 149.
Temple, the; 157.
Tenby; 38, 40.
Tendring, 57.
textiles; 31-32.
Thames; 41, 45, 48–50, 114, 117–118.
Thirty Years War; 17–18.
Thompson, one-eyed gunner; 85.
Tilbury; 49.
Tiptree Heath; 113.
torture; see atrocities.
Tower of London; 57, 157, 159.
Town Hall; 135.
townspeople; see civilians.
trade; 20, 31, 65, 67, 149.
trained bands; 36, 41, 49, 58.
treason; 66.
Treaty, Personal Treaty with the King; 35–36, 108–109, 119, 142, 144, 147, 152.
trenches; see fortifications.
trial, of the King; 11, 150, 155.
troops; see soldiers.
Tuke, Col. Samuel; 128.
Tuscany; 134-135, 138.

Uttoxeter; 123.

Vesey, Capt.; 58.
Vote of No Addresses; 29.

Wales; 37–38, 40, 43, 66, 71–74, 123, 144–145.
Waller, William; 17.
Walmer; 41, 74, 78, 114–115.
war crimes; 40, 53, 66, 94, 97, 148, 150, 157.
Ware; 28.
Warren, the; 78.
Warrington; 123.
Warwick Castle; 68.
Warwick, Earl of Lord Admiral; 67, 115, 118.
Warwick; 147.
Warwickshire; 67.
weather; 20, 58, 74, 87, 147, 149, 154.
weavers; 65.
West Country; 74.
West Indies; 10.
Westminster Hall; 36.
Westminster; 10, 34, 36, 43, 67, 70–71, 88, 104, 106, 108, 147, 152, 160.
Westmoreland; 123.
Whalley, Col; 45, 49, 137.
Wharton, Lord; 143.
Whitehall; 11, 151, 154.
Willoughby, Lord, 118.
Windsor; 40, 147, 151–152.
Winwick; 123.
Woolwich; 45.
Worcestershire; 67.
World War I; 19.
Wren, Matthew Bishop of Ely; 102.

Yarmouth, Great Yarmouth; 115–118.
Yorkshire; 166, 168.